Louis Albert Banks

The Honeycombs of Life

A Volume of Sermons and Addresses

Louis Albert Banks

The Honeycombs of Life
A Volume of Sermons and Addresses

ISBN/EAN: 9783743331150

Manufactured in Europe, USA, Canada, Australia, Japa

Cover: Foto ©ninafisch / pixelio.de

Manufactured and distributed by brebook publishing software (www.brebook.com)

Louis Albert Banks

The Honeycombs of Life

THE
HONEYCOMBS OF LIFE

A VOLUME OF

SERMONS AND ADDRESSES

BY

REV. LOUIS ALBERT BANKS, D.D.

AUTHOR OF "THE PEOPLE'S CHRIST" "WHITE SLAVES" "THE REVIVAL
QUIVER" "COMMON FOLKS' RELIGION" ETC.

PASTOR HANSON PLACE M. E. CHURCH, BROOKLYN, N.Y.

BOSTON
LEE AND SHEPARD PUBLISHERS
10 MILK STREET
1894

COPYRIGHT, 1894,
BY LEE AND SHEPARD.

THE HONEYCOMBS OF LIFE.

ELECTROTYPING BY C. J. PETERS & SON.

PRESSWORK BY S. J. PARKHILL & CO.

TO

MY FRIEND

The Honorable Edward Howard Dunn

WHOSE UNSELFISH FRIENDSHIP AND
BROTHERLY KINDNESS HAS BEEN A HONEYCOMB
OF ENCOURAGEMENT AND INSPIRATION

This Volume

IS AFFECTIONATELY DEDICATED

BY THE AUTHOR.

AUTHOR'S PREFACE

THE sermons and addresses in this volume have all been delivered during the past year in the regular course of my ministry in Boston and Brooklyn. They are reprinted here as delivered, without change. The direct style of the public address has been retained. The friends throughout the country who have so graciously received the volumes which have preceded this are responsible for the present publication. In selecting from the work of the year material for this volume, I have had in view the desire of presenting a diversity of topics and themes such as would fairly be representative of my work. The kind assurances which have come to me from multitudes of my brethren in the ministry in regard to the helpfulness of previous volumes, lead me to hope that to the preacher, the Sunday-school teacher, and Christian workers of every type, this new volume may, by illustration and suggestion, prove to be of some real profit. Sincerely hoping that every one who reads these discourses may find some honey that shall sweeten life's daily struggles and inspire to loftier exertions. I send them forth with a brother's blessing.

Louis Albert Banks.

Brooklyn, May 23, 1894.

CONTENTS

CHAPTER		PAGE
I.	The Honeycombs of Life	9
II.	Life in the King's Country	28
III.	A Wise Simplicity which outwits the Devil	49
IV.	The Soul's Resources	67
V.	An Earnest Life	90
VI.	Anxiety, Its Danger and Its Cure	109
VII.	What is It to be a Christian?	122
VIII.	At the Gate Beautiful	145
IX.	The Nobility of Service	162
X.	Lucy Stone: A Heroine of the Struggle for Human Rights	183
XI.	Fresh Bread for To-day's Hunger	204
XII.	A Glad Sight for Weary Eyes	219
XIII.	Our Brother in Yellow	236
XIV.	The Problem of Man-Flight	257
XV.	The Pilgrimage of Faith	276
XVI.	The Well-Diggers in the Valley of Baca	296

CHAPTER		PAGE
XVII.	AN ENTHUSIASM FOR HUMANITY	311
XVIII.	TALMAGE AND HIS WORK	315
XIX.	SPIRITUAL AND OTHER LESSONS FROM THE PRESIDENT'S INAUGURATION	323
XX.	JAMES RUSSELL LOWELL, THE POET-REFORMER	330
XXI.	WHITTIER AND THE GOLDEN RULE	336
XXII.	LUCY LARCOM AND HER SWEET SONGS OF COMMON LIFE	341
XXIII.	THE YACHT RACE AS A PICTURE OF HUMAN LIFE	348
XXIV.	A CROWN FOR THE MAN WHO FAILS . .	362
XXV.	THE COMING OF CHRIST'S KINGDOM IN NEW YORK	380

THE HONEYCOMBS OF LIFE

I

THE HONEYCOMBS OF LIFE

"He put forth the end of the rod that was in his hand, and dipped it in an honeycomb, and put his hand to his mouth; and his eyes were enlightened." — 1 SAM. xiv. 27.

AND this was the way it came about. The Israelites, under Saul, were encamped over against the Philistines. It was a period of discouragement for the army of Israel. Many Israelites, believing that Saul would be defeated in the threatened battle, had endeavored to "feather their own nest" by joining the camp of the enemy. Multitudes of others were hiding around in the hills, waiting to see which army would be victorious, and ready to cry "good Lord" or "good devil," as seemed most likely to save their own worthless heads. I am sorry to say that the representatives of that class are not all dead yet.

It was a gloomy spirit that hung about the camp of Israel, and something unusual was greatly needed to put heart and enthusiasm into the army. Jonathan, Saul's son, determined to make a heroic effort to break the courage of the enemy and arouse the enthusiasm of his own troops. I love Jonathan. The Old Testament has no more lovable character than he. Bishop Hall quaintly says that Jonathan was "a sweet imp out of a crab-stock." Jonathan called to his armor-bearer, and said, "Come, let us take our lives in our hands and go over to the enemy's garrison, and try what we can do to put them into confusion." He said nothing to anybody else about it; but these two went out, not simply as two reckless lads, but they went saying to themselves, "God can save by many or by few."

I have not time to tell the whole story, which is exceedingly interesting; but it was only a little while until this independent skirmishing of Jonathan's had put the whole Philistine army into confusion, and as they began to beat a hasty retreat, the Copperhead cowards saw it, and came trooping down from the hills, swelling Saul's army by many hundreds. The king prepared to pursue the Philistines; but before he did this, he made all his followers take an oath not to taste of food until the pursuit was over. Jonathan was not present when this oath was taken, and knew nothing of it. Along in the afternoon they came to a great wood, where the wild bees had taken the hollow trees for hives, and honey was abundant. The Israelites were nearly famished; but, remembering their solemn oath, not a man lifted his hand to his mouth. But Jonathan, not being bound by any such restrictions, coming under an overhanging limb full of honey, thrust the end of his rod into the comb, and breaking off a piece of it, began to eat of the delicious food, and as his hunger was appeased, he was refreshed in spirit, and his eyes brightened.

We have nothing to do with the further story, where only Jonathan's great personal popularity with the army saved his life. It is that wayside honeycomb waiting for the battle-worn and weary Jonathan, rich in the power to comfort and refresh him, and send him on with new vigor and courage — that is the picture I wish to study with you.

I

Let us consider some of the honeycombs of our common life, which are open to every one of us in times of weariness and need. Surely, when finding our theme in the life of Jonathan, we cannot fail to emphasize the fact that one of the sweetest of life's honeycombs is *friendship*.

There is nothing more beautiful in history than Jonathan's friendship for David. How delightfully unselfish it was! Jonathan was the heir apparent to his father's throne, himself a most heroic spirit, and universally beloved and popular. The first time he ever sees David is when he comes back from the death of Goliath, where the women are singing, —

"Saul hath slain his thousands,
And David his ten thousands."

From that hour the shepherd lad from Bethlehem stood in the light of a popular rival.

"Looking then upon him in his loveliness of person and of character, Jonathan saw with prophetic ken the sure future of David as the coming king of Israel, as the one in whose glowing light his own star of earthly hope must pale. But in the first flush of that discovery, there was no shade of envy, nor yet the faintest trace of regret in the more than royal heart of Jonathan." How splendid the picture stands out against all the intrigue and jealousy of Saul's court: "And it came to pass, when he had made an end of speaking unto Saul, that the soul of Jonathan was knit with the soul of David, and Jonathan loved him as his own soul." From that time forward, every heart-throb of Jonathan's friendship for David was a heart-throb of unselfish devotion to him to whom he was a friend. Death itself could not break that bond. When David found Jonathan dead on his last battle-field, his heart-cry of sorrow for his lost friend was: —

"I am distressed for thee, my brother Jonathan:
Very pleasant hast thou been unto me:
Thy love to me was wonderful,
Passing the love of women."

Long years afterward, when David was settled firmly on his throne, he asked of those about him, "Is there yet any that is left of the house of Saul, that I may show him kindness for Jonathan's sake?" and the crippled Mephibosheth was lifted out of poverty and given the seat of honor at the king's table in proof of the unchangeableness of David's friendship for Jonathan.

The Bible idea of friendship throughout is the love which loves for the very joy of loving, without reckoning up the measure of return. Moses says to Israel, "The Lord did not set his love upon you because ye were more in number than any people; for ye were the fewest of all people: but because the Lord loved you." Some of our poets sing this thought very sweetly. Whittier says, —

> "Love is sweet in any guise;
> But its best is sacrifice.
>
> He who giving does not crave,
> Likest is to Him who gave
> Life itself the loved to save."

Helen Hunt Jackson sings, —

> "When love is strong,
> It never tarries to take heed

Or know if its return exceed
Its gifts; in its sweet haste no greed,
No strife belong.

It hardly asks
If it be loved at all; to take
So barren seems, when it can make
Such bliss, for the beloved's sake,
Of bitter tasks."

George Eliot adds her testimony, —

"So if I live or die to serve my friend,
'Tis for my love, — 'tis for my friend alone,
And not for any rate that friendship bears
In heaven or in earth."

The highest honor put on any man in the Old Testament is when Abraham is called "the friend of God." The most comforting thing Jesus could conceive of to say to the disciples before leaving them was, "No longer do I call you servants . . . but I have called you friends."

Mrs. Margaret Sangster, who says so many things which are rich in their knowledge of the human heart, declares that there is no finer test of what a man really is than the way in which he makes and keeps his friends. In the first early bloom of life friends are easily won and often as easily lost. The youth at school, or the maiden in her teens, wears often the rose of friendship as a lady dressed for a party wears a rose upon her bosom. It is prized while it is fresh; but, as the heat and dust of the swift hours cause it to wilt, it is cast aside without a pang. Some other flower will take its place; there are so many other flowers ready to one's hand in the bright gardens of youth. But later on, when our powers have in some sort arrived at maturity, and the simplest acts are infused with a deeper and sterner meaning than lies on the surface, men and women grow into a truer appreciation of the value and worth of friends and friendships.

Those who have been by our side alike in our joys and sorrows, are to us as precious gems, to be treasured in the safest places of our love and care. We regard them with something of the reverent affection that a soldier feels for the decoration on his breast. A jewel to be guarded and delighted in, a sign of promotion, a gauge of merit, is a friend in whom one confides without a shadow of a doubt.

Be true to your friends. Nothing in this vale of humanity is in the long run so good an investment as friendship, human and divine. Solomon says, —

"A friend loveth at all times,
And a brother is born for adversity."

"Ointment and perfume rejoice the heart:
So doth the sweetness of a man's friend that cometh of hearty counsel.
Thine own friend, and thy father's friend, forsake not."

"Iron sharpeneth iron;
So a man sharpeneth the countenance of his friend."

And One greater than Solomon has said: "Greater love hath no man than this, that a man lay down his life for his friends" — as friendship has many a time prompted a man to do gladly.

Cultivate the gift of friendship that is within you. You have no other talent that will draw higher interest in the social market-place. Jeremy Taylor says: "A friend shares my sorrow and makes it but a moiety; but he swells my joy and makes it double." Rest assured, my brother, that, —

"A friend is worth all hazards we can run.
Poor is the friendless master of the world:
A world in purchase of a friend is gain."

Here is a honeycomb possible for us all, and one that will endure to the end. Dr. H. Clay Trumbull, who wrote that beautiful book, " Friendship the Master-Passion," and who testifies as an expert on the subject of friendship, shows by scholarly argument that the word translated " charity " in the Old Version, and " love " in the Revised Version, of the thirteenth chapter of First Corinthians, should be translated friendship-love. Let us apply the glowing words of Paul to ourselves this morning. " If I speak with the tongues of men and of angels, but have not friendship-love, I am become sounding brass, or a clanging cymbal. And if I have the gift of prophecy, and know all mysteries and all knowledge; and if I have all faith, so as to remove mountains, but have not friendship-love, I am nothing. And if I bestow all my goods to feed the poor, and if I give my body to be burned, but have not friendship-love, it profiteth me nothing. Friendship-love suffereth long, and is kind; friendship-love envieth not; friendship-love vaunteth not itself, is not puffed up, doth not behave itself unseemly, seeketh not its own, is not provoked, taketh not account of evil; rejoiceth not in unrighteousness, but rejoiceth with the truth; beareth all things, believeth all things, hopeth all things, endureth all things. Friendship-love never faileth: but whether there be prophecies, they shall be done away; whether there be tongues, they shall cease; whether there be knowledge, it shall be done away. . . . But now abideth faith, hope, friendship-love, these three; and the greatest of these is friendship-love."

II

Another honeycomb, open to us all, is a *cheerful heart*. The London *Christian World*, some time ago, had an article of marked ability on "Ministering Gladness," in which the writer took the ground that, if joy is not the main end of life, it is certainly life's ordained condition. Surely no life is healthy without it. It may be true that enjoyment must ever elude those who live for nothing else: but it is equally true that God has made life and joy so inseparable that no one can be healthy and noble without also being glad, sooner or later, and without coming, finally, to rejoice much more than to grieve. So to speak, the happy God has taken pains to make His creatures happy too. The chief ordinances of nature bear witness to this. Maternal pain, as a rule, bears no comparison with maternal exultation. Healthy children, with a fair amount of food and kindness, know far more joy than sorrow. Thousands of invalids who never expect to be well again in this world are patterns of permanent cheerfulness and perennial fountains of gladness to all about them. One of the most, if not the most, cheerful-hearted and happy of the children with whom I ever came in contact is Helen Keller, who has been since early childhood deaf and dumb and blind. Indeed, one of the gladdest schools I have ever seen in my life was an institution for the blind. In ordinary cases, the reason why we so cry out under pain is because we are not used to it. Commonly everything we do ministers to our happiness. We are glad to go to bed when weary; glad to rise refreshed to salute a new day; and glad to go about life's ordinary duties while the sun is in the heavens. Seeing, hearing, smelling, tasting, and feeling are so many open inlets to the ordained joy of simply being alive. Every season brings its own especial gladness, every climate has its peculiar delights. Not only so, but to the consciousness of present enjoyment is to be added the pleasures of memory, and the felicities of hope, together with the marvellous power we possess of dwelling lightly on past pain, while reviving and re-enjoying bygone mercies, all of which means that the loving Creator has, with the most far-reaching foresight and minutely adjusted skill, strung our very beings to the music of good cheer.

There is no real exception to the divine ordinance of predominant joy. There is pain. There are woes innumerable. Some lives are unspeakably sad. The very Saviour of the world is known as "the Man of Sorrows." But we no sooner recall this fact, than the gloom begins to break. It was "for the joy that was set before him" that the Son of God "endured the cross." Sorrow, then, need only be temporary. It is the shadow of joy. It is, therefore, also prophetic: "Blessed are they that mourn: for they shall be comforted."

Pain is a necessary discipline. Jehovah "doth not afflict willingly, nor grieve the children of men." This necessary discipline implies only the deep love of our Heavenly Father. The goodness of God leadeth to repentance. Christ was anointed to heal the broken-hearted. The Gospel proclaimers are bringers of good tidings, whose rapid feet are beautiful upon the mountains. The first church — that which was born in Jerusalem on Pentecost — held daily festival; when Philip went down to Samaria there was "great joy in that city," and the chief reason why the first preachers " turned the world upside down," was because they everywhere made dull lives bright, and turned sighs into singing. Along this line of joy-bringing ministry lies at this day the highest duty of the church, because therein is to be found the most crying need of the world. Even the most callous of men probably need to be encouraged to call to mind their sins as not past forgiveness; while enormous numbers of the masses urgently require strong and generous help to win them back from despair, and convince them that God is love, and Calvary the natural manifestation of His great-hearted tenderness for us. Open the honeycomb of your cheerful heart, my brother, to the weary and discouraged.

III

The only other honeycomb that I shall speak of this morning is made in the same hive with the last — *a hope in Christ*. This, too, with all its treasured sweetness, is open to every one. Hope is a part of our divine inheritance. Experience discovers many cheats and destroys many ideals, but it has not been able to destroy hope. We have all been deceived many times, and found the hook neatly hidden within the most attractive bait; but though the bait changes as we grow older, hope still lures us onward.

Our world is so marvellously constructed, and we are so placed in it, that the future always seems to be beautiful, and every year cheers the heart with a new promise. No doubt, the final intention of God in ever luring us onward by hopes which are forever eluding us, is to show us that nothing on earth is permanent, and that when we have completed this life another one awaits us. There was one bird-song that Thoreau had heard many times, and though he tried every time he heard it to find the singer, he never succeeded. He travelled far and fast, but never caught sight of its flight or its rest. Through all these years we have heard one song, sweeter than any bird-note, but we have never caught a glimpse of the singer. In our search we have seen and heard many other things of beauty and interest, but not this one. This is a messenger sent by the Heavenly Father to entice us away from the meadows and groves of earth, toward the fields and forests of a still brighter and more glorious land.

Even here and now, hope tunes the soul to the sweet strains of heavenly music. There is an interesting story of Ole Bull and Ericsson, the inventor. They were friends in early life, but drifted apart, and did not meet again until each had become famous. Bull had charmed the ears of admiring thousands all over the civilized world, while the part the great mechanician played in naval warfare during the war roused the North to enthusiasm, and startled the world. When taking his leave, Bull invited

Ericsson to attend his concert that night. Ericsson, however, declined, saying that he had no time to waste.

Their acquaintance being thus renewed, Bull continued to call on his old friend when visiting New York, and usually, when taking his leave, would ask Ericsson to attend his concert; but Ericsson always declined the invitation.

Upon one occasion, Bull pressed him urgently, and said, —

"If you do not come, I shall bring my violin here and play in your shop.".

"If you bring the thing here, I shall smash it."

Here were two men, the very opposite of each other — Bull, an impulsive, romantic dreamer; Ericsson, stern, thoughtful, practical, improving every moment with mathematical precision.

Bull's curiosity was aroused to know what effect music would have upon the grim matter-of-fact man of squares and circles. So, taking his violin with him, he went to Ericsson's shop. He had removed the strings, screws, and apron. Noticing a displeased expression on Ericsson's face, Bull called his attention to certain defects in the instrument, and, speaking of its construction, asked Ericsson about the scientific and acoustic properties involved in the grain of certain woods. From this he passed on to a discussion of sound-waves, semi-tones, etc.

To illustrate his meaning, he replaced the string, and, improvising a few chords, drifted into a rich melody.

The workmen, charmed, dropped their tools and stood in silent wonder.

He played on and on; and, when he finally ceased, Ericsson raised his bowed head, and with moist eyes said: —

"Do not stop. Go on! Go on! I never knew until now what there was lacking in my life."

So many men and women go on for years and years imagining that religion is something sentimental and impracticable — a thing for dreamers — that they do not need it, or care for it, until God manages in some unexpected way to carry the sweet hope of the Gospel into their hearts. Then, with wet eyes and tender hearts, they exclaim, "I never knew until now what there was lacking in my life!" I covet for you, every one, a life fed with honey and the honeycomb here, and abundant entrance into that land where our fondest hopes shall be lost in glorious fruition.

II

LIFE IN THE KING'S COUNTRY

"The King's country." — ACTS xii. 20.

IT is related of Hugh Latimer that when he was to preach one day before Henry VIII., he stood up in the pulpit, and, beholding the king, he addressed himself in a kind of soliloquy thus: "Latimer, Latimer, Latimer, take care what you say, for the great king Henry VIII. is here." Then he paused, with all eyes upon him, and with tones of still deeper awe exclaimed: "Latimer, Latimer, Latimer, take care what you say, for the great King of kings is here." Slowly but surely there is being built up in the midst of this world a spiritual kingdom — the kingdom of our Lord Jesus Christ. It is an invisible kingdom to the eye of sense, but all the more real because of that, for it is the unseen that is eternal and immutable. From out our dusty streets, from the busy marts of toil, they are being gathered one by one; without reference to earthly distinction, from rich and from poor, from learned and from ignorant, from black and from white, the great work of spiritual naturalization is going on. Paul said of himself and his friends, "Our citizenship is in heaven." So all around the globe the numbers are multiplying from among Americans, Englishmen, Frenchmen, Germans, Russians, Chinese, Japanese, and from every monarchy or republic and nearly every tribe among the sons of men, of those who are taking the oath of allegiance to Him who is King of kings and Lord of lords.

The great mission of the Christian church is to win aliens to this holy citizenship. The King's country, in this high sense in which we study it, pervades the universal consciousness of man. Its domain is the moral and spiritual life of mankind. The possibilities of citizenship in this heavenly dominion is within every human soul. We carry in our own hearts, by the very charter of our creation, made as we are in the likeness and image of God, credentials which, if presented with penitence and faith, will admit us into the high fellowship of the citizens of the King's country. Let us study some of the characteristics of life in this spiritual dominion.

Henri Amiel says, "Every soul has a climate of its own, or rather is a climate." And this is peculiarly true of Christ. He creates a spiritual climate, the atmosphere of which is breathed and enjoyed by all His disciples. For to be a Christian is to be like Christ. "Come unto me," He says, "all ye that labor and are heavy laden, and I will give you rest. Take my yoke upon you, and learn of me; for I am meek and lowly in heart: and ye shall find rest unto your souls. For my yoke is easy, and my burden is light." Again He says, "For I have given you an example, that ye should do as I have done to you." And Paul says, "Let this mind be in you, which was also in Christ Jesus." And Peter tells us, "But as he which hath called you is holy, so be ye holy in all manner of conversation." And still again Peter urges, "For even hereunto were ye called: because Christ also suffered for us, leaving us an example, that ye should follow his steps." And John declares, "He that saith he abideth in him ought himself also so to walk. even as he walked." These Scriptures, in perfect harmony with the universal teaching of the Bible, make Christ the very centre around which His whole spiritual dominion is to revolve. In John's vision of the New Jerusalem, one great characteristic was that they did not need the light of the sun or the moon, but the Lord God was the light of it, which is only the fulfilment of that great prophecy of Isaiah, who declares that the influence of the great Redeemer shall work marvellous transformations in the earth, until He Himself shall be the central sun of an all-encompassing kingdom. The glorious promise reads. "For brass I will bring gold, and for iron I will bring silver, and for wood brass, and for stones iron. I will also make thy officers peace. and thine exactors righteousness. Violence shall no more be heard in thy land. wasting nor destruction within thy borders; but thou shalt call thy walls Salvation and thy gates Praise. The sun shall be no more thy light by day; neither for brightness shall the moon give light unto thee:

but the Lord shall be unto thee an everlasting light, and thy God thy glory. Thy sun shall no more go down: neither shall thy moon withdraw itself: for the Lord shall be thine everlasting light, and the days of thy mourning shall be ended."

Susan Coolidge, thinking about Christ as the central sun, creating as He does a spiritual climate for human souls to dwell in, sings a most helpful lay : —

"O heart beloved, O kindest heart!
 Balming like summer and like sun
 The sting of tears, the ache of sorrow,
 The shy, cold hurts which sting and smart,
 The frets and cares which underrun
 The dull day and the dreaded morrow —
 How when thou comest all turns fair,
 Hard things seem possible to bear,
 Dark things less dark, if thou art there.

 Thou keepest a climate of thine own
 'Mid earth's wild weather and gray skies,
 A soft, still air for human breathing,
 A genial, all-embracing zone,
 Where frosts smite not nor winds arise ;
 And past the tempest-storm of feeling
 Each grieved and weak and weary thing,
 Each bird with numbed and frozen wing,
 May sink to rest and learn to sing.

> Like some cathedral stone begirt,
> Which keeps through change of cold and heat
> Still temperature and equal weather,
> Thy sweetness stands, untouched, unhurt,
> By any mortal storms that beat, —
> Calm, helpful, undisturbed forever."

One of the great characteristics of the King's country is the consciousness of God's presence in human life. Two little children, Grace and Rob, were very much interested in their beautiful new Christmas books. Grace, the elder of the two, was explaining to Rob what a wonderfully good and generous person Santa Claus was. Rob was becoming impressed more and more favorably. Finally he asked, "Where does he live?" Assuming a most knowing look, Grace replied, "Well, Rob, I don't 'xactly know, but I guess right across from God." It is the glory of the people who live in the King's country that the sunlight of God's presence falls daily upon their lives. Not that there are not trials in the King's country, not that there are not hard experiences of discipline; but for every day of storm there is a bow of promise. There is a parable that tells how Laughter and Tears met one day in a shady lane. The sunshine and shade mingled pleasantly there, and the breath of the woods was strong in the air, as was also the fragrance of the clover-field near by; but the lane was all too narrow to allow both to pass, for Laughter was full of life and buoyancy, and romped about so much that he took up a deal of room, while Tears seemed to be half blind, and could scarcely see her way.

She said in a soft, plaintive voice, like the song of a night bird, "Why don't you let me pass? This is my path."

"No," replied Laughter, "this lane is mine; and I am in a hurry, so you'd better climb the fence into the dark wood, and walk through the dead leaves."

"Why don't you climb the other fence?" said Tears, softly, "and run along through the clover in the sunshine? I am sure you'd like it better."

"Well," rejoined Laughter pleasantly, "I am sure I don't want to quarrel with so gentle a maiden; and so, as we don't seem to agree about the path, suppose I turn about and go with you?"

So they went on together through the twink-

ling shine and shadow, and each felt better for
the company of the other. And that is why,
says the fable, that whenever you meet Tears,
Laughter is not far away.

But upon far more solid grounds than any
pleasant fable rests the assurance that to the
citizen of the King's country the silver lining
of divine care shall glorify every cloud, and
at every eventide there shall be light. Even
in the deepest trials that can come to human
hearts, the King's country has peace and hope.

A Western secular journal contained the
other day a most touching little incident. In
the city where this newspaper is published
there was a family consisting of husband and
wife and one little boy scarcely old enough to
talk plainly. A few weeks ago the young wife
and mother was stricken down to die. It was
so sudden, so dreadful, when the grave family
physician called them together in the parlor,
and in his solemn, professional way intimated to
them the truth — there was no hope. Then the
question arose among them, Who would tell
her? Not the doctor! It would be cruel to
let the man of science go to their dear one on

such an errand. Not the aged mother, who was to be left childless and alone! Not the young husband, who was walking the floor with clinched hands and rebellious heart! Not — there was only one other; and at this moment he looked up from the book he had been playing with, unnoticed by them all, and asked gravely, —

"Is my mamma doin' to die?"

Then, without waiting for an answer, he sped from the room, and up-stairs as fast as his little feet would carry him. Friends and neighbors were watching by the sick one. They wonderingly noticed the pale face of the child as he climbed on the bed and laid his small head on his mother's pillow.

"Mamma," he asked in sweet, caressing tones, "is you 'fraid to die?"

The woman looked at him with swift intelligence. Perhaps she had been thinking of this.

"Who told you, Charlie?" she asked faintly.

"Doctor an' papa an' gamma — everybody," he whispered.

"Mamma, dear 'ittle mamma, doan' be 'fraid to die, 'ill you?"

"No, Charlie," said the young mother, after one supreme pang of grief, "no; mamma won't be afraid."

"Jus' shut your eyes in 'e dark, mamma; teep hold my hand, an' when you open 'em, mamma, it'll be all light there."

When the family gathered awe-stricken at the bedside, Charlie held up his little hand.

"Hush! My mamma's doin' to sleep. Her won't wake up here any more."

And so it proved. There was no heart-rending farewell, no agony of parting; for when the young mother woke she had passed beyond, and, as Baby Charlie said, "It was all light there."

So every dweller in the King's country shall find the light stronger than the darkness. As Susan Coolidge sings again:—

"Grief is strong, but joy is stronger;
Night is long, but day is longer;
When life's riddle solves and clears,
And the angels in our ears
Whisper the sweet answer low
(Answer full of love and blessing),
How our wonderment will grow
At the blindness of our guessing.
All the hard things we recall,
Made so easy — after all.

Earth is sweet, but heaven is sweeter;
Love complete, but faith completer;
Close beside our wandering ways,
Through dark nights and weary days,
Stand the angels with bright eyes;
And the shadow of the cross
Falls upon and sanctifies
All our pains and all our loss;
Though we stumble, though we fall,
God is helping — after all.

Sigh, then, soul, but sing in sighing,
To the happier things replying;
Dry the tears that dim thy seeing,
Give glad thoughts for life and being;
Time is but the little entry
To eternity's large dwelling;
And the heavenly guards keep sentry,
Urging, guiding, half compelling;
Till, the puzzling way quite past,
Thou shalt enter in at last."

The atmosphere of the King's country is one of reverence and thanksgiving. Conscience is master there, but not a morbid or despairing conscience. Instead, a conscience comforted by the assurance of divine sympathy and love. The psalms of David contain the spiritual biography of an intense nature, who, through great trials and sorrows, scarred and wounded by many sins, came at last to dwell in peace in the

King's country. What splendid strains sometimes swell out from David's harp, when his soul is exalted at the thought of the transformation God has wrought in him, a sinful, erring, weak man; when he reflects on the power that has brought him back to the delicious, childlike feeling of trust and joy and love, in which he is cleansed from the dirt and stain of bitter warfare with temptation and sin, and finds himself at last rejoicing in the heavenly communion! There is nothing grander in human language than some of these outbursts. Hear one of them; I am sure it will tell the story of many other lives: "I waited patiently for the Lord; and he inclined unto me, and heard my cry. He brought me up also out of an horrible pit, out of the miry clay, and set my feet upon a rock, and established my goings. And he hath put a new song in my mouth, even praise unto our God."

Let us cherish as we would life itself, for it is more valuable than life, that sensitiveness and tenderness of conscience that is characteristic of life in the King's country.

In Coleridge's story of the "Ancient Mariner"

we read how the captain of a ship shot an albatross that had followed them through a long and prosperous voyage, after which the wind ceased to blow, and the ship stood still in a dead calm under the equator, until death relieved the sufferings of all the crew. In their superstition they attributed these sufferings to the shooting of the albatross, and, in token of their bitter resentment, they hung the dead bird around the captain's neck as a punishment. Whatever may be the meaning the poet intended, it is surely true that conscience, like a bird of hope, guides safely the human life so long as she is cherished and obeyed; but conscience wounded and dead means a body of death and despair around the neck of its murderer. It does not appear from Coleridge's poem that there was any enmity toward the albatross on the part of the captain; it was a mere wanton use of his cross-bow because the bird presented the nearest object for his skill. Alas! is it not true that men sometimes shoot and kill, in mere thoughtlessness, the conscience that is the best friend and guide of life? You that would be dwellers in the

King's country, cherish with every possible tenderness the record of Himself which God has put in your breast.

Service is the standard of honor in the King's country. The Master said that the standard among His disciples should be entirely different from that of the world. The world honors the strongest, the richest, the successful, and they are the ones who are waited upon and served and ministered to. But Christ declares that in the King's country the greatest is the one who is the greatest servant. "Whosoever of you will be the chiefest, shall be servant of all."

One may trace the frontiers of the King's country in every land, in every town and city, in every social circle, in every home, by the exhibition, or the lack of it, of this spirit of brotherly service. How it glorifies all common life where it prevails! The other day, in one of our cities, two small boys signalled a street-car. When the car stopped, it was noticed that one boy was lame. With much solicitude the other boy helped the cripple aboard, and, after telling the conductor to go ahead, returned to the sidewalk. The lame boy braced himself up in his seat so that he could look out of the car window, and the other passengers observed that at intervals the little fellow would wave his hand and smile. Following the direction of his glances, the passengers saw the other boy running along the sidewalk, straining every muscle to keep up with the car. They watched his pantomime in silence for a few blocks, and then a gentleman asked the lame boy who the other boy was. "My brother," was the prompt reply. "Why does he not ride with you in the car?" was the next question. "Because he hasn't any money." answered the lame boy sorrowfully. But the little runner — running that his crippled brother might ride — had a face in which sorrow had no part, only the gladness of a self-denying soul. O my brother, you who long to do great service for the King and reach life's noblest triumph, here is your picture — willing to run that the crippled lives may ride, willing to bear one another's burdens, and so fulfil the law of Christ — that is the spirit of the King's country.

All about us are men and women who are

being swallowed up in temptation and sin, whom we can save if that divine spirit of service possess our souls. Did you ever see the firemen, when rescuing men and women from the burning building, and the ladder would not reach those that were in peril, when, in the dreadful emergency, a fireman stood on the top rung of the ladder, added his own length, and made of himself a human ladder, over which the imperilled men and women climbed down into safety? Often brave firemen have done that. So, brothers, if you and I shall breathe in its purity the atmosphere of the King's country, we shall with all joy bare our shoulders to carry the burdens of the tempted and weak.

In this divine atmosphere of the Christ-land, it is possible to have the sweetest fellowships that human souls may know. Some one well says that fellowship is something too precious to be built merely upon a common study or a common taste. The foundations needed for such a temple are nothing short of character, reverence, and love. The college friend, or even the messmate of the camp, if he have drifted into habits gross and carnal, can find in the association no more than a momentary tie connecting him with the old-time friend whose character has grown more spiritual through the years. All the symbolism of the lodge, all the charms of a common secret and a common interest, cannot make real brothers of men who have contrasted moral codes, or opposed conceptions of duty, or antagonistic hopes about the life to come. All other fellowships are artificial and found to be perishable; but Christian fellowship is founded in common character and a common love, and is more lasting than life itself.

This Christian fellowship, which we may well thank God is more common in the world to-day than ever before, does not depend upon unity of creed, but upon a harmony of spirit, of life motive — a unity in high and holy purpose. The Roman bishop in his purple gown, or the Salvation Army captain in his red shirt, may neither of them agree with me in creed; but if under the purple gown and the red shirt there be found warm hearts beating in loyalty to the Lord Jesus Christ, bowing in reverence at the foot of the Cross, seeing in all men their brothers, and giving themselves in glad service to cure the world's sorrows — then neither gown nor shirt nor lack of creed can keep us three from being brothers in the King's country. We have seen a most remarkable illustration of this during the past week, when, on the platform of the Brooklyn Tabernacle, Calvinist and Arminian, Jew and Gentile, Catholic and Protestant, all united in words of fellowship and fraternal greeting to a fellow-worker for the glory of God and the uplifting of humanity. Such scenes give us hope and inspire us to believe the glorious promises of our blessed faith.

Brothers and sisters, I have tried to tell you a little about life in the King's country. But I cannot close without putting a personal, definite question to your own soul. Let it come to each one of you as though we two were here alone, and I God's messenger to you. Art thou in the King's country? If you must give the answer in the negative, let me entreat you to stay no longer outside. An old age and death outside of hope in Christ is the saddest conception of the human mind. One of our modern painters has given us a striking picture which he calls Death in the Desert. Upon the canvas is seen in the foreground a dying camel, lying in the midst of a desert of burning sand. The blazing sun shimmers in the midst of a heaven of glowing brass. There is not a leaf or blade visible from horizon to horizon; but the poor creature, which has been abandoned by some passing caravan, lifts a feeble head to look up toward that sky, through which the multitudes of impatient vultures are winging their way to the expected feast of death. This sad and awful picture suggests the fate of many a man who, rejecting the hope in Christ and hardening his heart against the mercy of God, drops out of life's caravan at last to die in the desert of despair. God forbid that it prove to be your picture! It need not be. Let us open the pages of Isaiah and look on a very different picture. The scene is that of a royal garden, such as the old kings of Judah planted on the slopes of Zion. And in the centre of its roses and its fountains there stands a great dovecote, with its innumerable windows for their various nests. And now at eventide from every quarter of the heavens we behold the multitude of doves winging their happy flight toward the loved abode. O my brother, when the flight of life is over and the storm of death threatens, you may find a happy home in the dovecote in the King's garden. Ah, but, says some discouraged soul, I have been going wrong, and instead of being in the King's country to-night, I am in the "far country" with the husks and the swine. What can be done for me? I thank God, if you are willing to leave the husks and the swine, we have a light to put in the window for you to-night. I have heard of a miner who was lost in a mine. The more he walked the deeper he seemed to get into its depths, and he became almost ready to give up in despair. Suddenly, when ready to abandon all hope, he thought he saw a faint light. He went toward it, it grew larger and larger, and immediately he walked out upon the greensward in the bright sunshine. My brother, I hold out to you the bright light of God's love. If you will follow it, no matter if only with trembling steps, it will bring you into the clear sunshine of a full salvation. I entreat you that you do not rest until your heart is the abode of the King.

> "Though Christ a thousand times
> In Bethlehem be born,
> If He's not born in thee,
> Thy soul is still forlorn.
> The cross on Golgotha
> Will never save thy soul;
> The cross in thine own heart
> Alone can make thee whole."

III

A WISE SIMPLICITY WHICH OUTWITS THE DEVIL

"I would have you wise unto that which is good, and simple concerning evil. And the God of peace shall bruise Satan under your feet shortly". — Rom. xvi. 19, 20.

THIS plain, straightforward declaration of Paul reminds us at once of his similar words to the church in Corinth, "In malice be children, but in understanding be men;" and both utterances send us back to Christ, and we hear Him saying to the disciples: "Behold, I send you forth as sheep in the midst of wolves: be ye therefore wise as serpents, and harmless as doves."

The plain, simple teaching of our text is: —

I.

That we are to be wise in all good things. To be, as Matthew Henry says, "skilful and intelligent in the truth and ways of God." If our Master's significant words, "Be ye therefore wise as serpents," mean anything, they clearly indicate that we are by no means to take leave of our common sense when we become Christians, or enter upon Christian work. There is need of all the practical wisdom within our power to attain, in our life of adherence to good truths, good duties, and good people, lest we be imposed upon or deluded.

"Wise but harmless" in every good cause is the Christian's motto. A herd of five thousand beeves were toiling over a lonely trail from New Mexico to Kansas, leaving behind them, across the plains and valleys, a swath as bare as if it had been swept by the fiery breath of a simoom. Suddenly the leader of the herd, a huge steer, started back in terror, gave vent to a snort of warning, and moved to the right and passed on. Those immediately in his rear turned to right or left, and their example was followed by each long-horned pilgrim as he reached the dreaded spot. When the entire herd had passed, a wide, trampled track lay behind, but near the middle of this dusty space stood a luxuriant island of grass three feet in diameter. A herdsman rode up to the spot and dismounted, expecting to find a rattlesnake, a creature of which cattle as well as horses have a well-founded dread. Instead of a serpent, however, the grass tuft contained only a harmless kildee plover, covering her nest, while her wings were kept in constant and violent motion. Seen indistinctly through the grass she had evidently been mistaken by the steer for a rattlesnake. She did not take flight even at the cowboy, but valiantly pecked at his boot as he gently pushed her one side to find that the nest contained four unfledged kildees. In the story of the little bird you have illustrated the wisdom of the serpent and the harmlessness of the dove.

It seems strange, when we reflect upon it, that it should need such continued emphasis to make people understand and appreciate the necessity of applying as much stern common sense to the conduct of the spiritual life, and the management of the campaign against sin, as they are wont to exercise in secular affairs. It is exceedingly hard to rub into the consciousness of many good people that, when the every-day world of business and society is illuminated by electricity, travels by Pullman car and palatial steamship, converses by telephone and ocean cable, and reads hourly editions of its favorite journal, the church cannot keep pace in influence and power with a tallow dip or ox team. In seeking to spread the reign of Jesus Christ over the hearts and lives of men, we must be true to our own time, "serve our own generation," approach men and women in the language which is common to their ear. How well Jesus Christ understood this: "No man putteth new wine into old wine-skins: else the new wine will burst the skins, and itself will be spilled, and the wine perisheth, and the skins: but they put new wine into fresh wine-skins, and both are preserved."

There is such a thing as "new wine." God's order of progress has not been revoked. The church of our time has its own mission; and, with God-given intuition, must evolve its own methods as truly as did the church in the days of the apostles, or of Luther, or of the Wesleys. Christianity is an ever-living force among living men; and we must, with reverent hearts and hands, but with the daring of our noble birthright as the "sons of God," forever adjust our methods to providences. In the language of Jesus, we must "discern the signs of the times." "The common people are as ready to hear God's word to-day as ever in the history of the world, and as open of heart and as quick to respond, if we adapt ourselves to the situation and get their ear by speaking their tongue with a sympathetic brother's face behind it" (Pentecost).

George Macdonald, the novelist preacher of England, tells in his book entitled "Robert Falconer," the story of the contrition of a soiled soul. Falconer was reading the story of the Magdalene to a company of ordinary, prosaic sinners. Some one sobbed. It was a young, slender girl, with a face disfigured by smallpox, and, save for the tearful look it wore, poor and expressionless. Falconer said something gentle to her.

"Will He ever come again?"

"Who?" said Falconer.

"Him — Jesus Christ. I've heard tell, I think, that He was to come again some day."

"Why do you ask?"

"Because," — she said, with a fresh burst of tears, which rendered her words that followed unintelligible. But she recovered herself in a few moments, and, as if finishing her sentence, put her hand up to her poor, thin, colorless hair, and said: —

"*My hair ain't long enough to wipe His feet.*"

Oh, let us not forget that we are disciples of Him who came to seek and to save the lost, and not be above the planning and devising of wise methods which will accomplish the great commission given us by the Master. Wise to save a lost soul, as we are to save a child lost in the swamp, or a man lost overboard — that is what I plead for.

Mrs. Farningham sings it with great clearness and power: —

> "A man was in the sea,
> How came he there?
> Only the foolish asked;
> The pressing care
> Was how to get him safely
> To the land—
> Not one but longed to stretch
> A helpful hand.

SIMPLICITY WHICH OUTWITS THE DEVIL

The pitiless sea
  Against one half-spent man!
The mocking water hissed,
  The wild waves ran;
The winds laughed in his ears,
  The unfriendly cloud
Beat him with raindrops
  Cruel, cold, and loud.

A hundred would have risked
  Their lives for him;
A thousand anxious eyes
  Were strained and dim;
And helpless hands were wrung,
  And prayers were cried, —
And still the desperate man
  Fought with the tide!

They could not launch a boat
  So fierce the wave —
Yet they could help the man
  Himself to save.
And buoy and rope and rocket
  Were at hand, —
At last, just living,
  He was drawn to land.

It was a crowd of brothers.
  A great cheer
Of thankful joy was raised,
  And many a tear
Stole down rough cheeks;
  And yet a stranger he!
What filled that throng
  With wild and thankful glee?

And he was only one!
  Why all this care?
Oh! round us is a sea
  Of dark despair;
Not one, but many men
  Are struggling there.
Listen! and you must hear
  Their breathless prayer!

He was a man, you say,
  That was enough!
But there are also men
  Who, in the rough
And surging waters
  Of our restless life,
Are beaten, bruised, half-drowned
  In the great strife!

Oh, foolish men to care
  So much for one,
And not care for the many!
  Let the sun
Of God's light wake your hearts,
  And make you wise
To see what is so plain
  Before your eyes.

The men are in the sea,
  Throw them a rope;
Watch them with pity,
  Give them words of hope.
They may be saved
  By some strong brother's hand.
They are Christ's men,
  Oh, draw them safe to land!"

II.

But there is only half of our message. While we are to be wise in that which is good, we are to be "simple concerning evil," "harmless as doves," and "in malice" are to be like "children." As one says, we are to be "so wise as not to be deceived, and yet so simple as not to be deceivers. It is a holy simplicity, not to be able to contrive, or palliate, or carry on any evil design." This Scripture is a sharp stab to the very heart of that Jesuitical proverb, "The end justifies the means." We are to conduct the campaign for righteousness in a frank, open-hearted way that does not depend in the slightest upon chicanery or trickery, but on straightforward justice and right.

The editor of the *Outlook* very clearly sets forth this idea: "There are two qualities which are constantly coming to light in connection with almost every misunderstanding or disagreement among bodies of men who are working together for a common end. When such men fall out, it will generally be found that there has been, on the part of somebody, lack of courage or lack of frankness. Sometimes sharp differences of view oblige men to separate and form new combinations; but the great majority of differences which arise between those who are working together are due to somebody's lack of courage and frankness. There is only one sound and wise way of managing common interests, and that is the way of absolute courage and frankness. If a group of men are to be controlled, it ought to be done by the methods of the statesman, not by those of the politician; by force of ideas and vigor of presentation, rather than by avoidance of open discussion and by those private agreements which degenerate into intrigues. We are constantly tempted to distrust our fellows, and to seek to accomplish the things we have at heart by placating individuals and trying to bring them to support our views privately, instead of courageously trusting the good sense of others, frankly stating the thing we want done, and relying upon the validity of ideas and the force of the presentment to carry out our ends. It is a great blunder to manage a body of men by any method which lacks frankness and candor. In the long run, such a method is certain to undermine the position of the man who uses it, and to bring down upon his head the structure which he has so carefully put together. The man who lacks frankness in dealing with other men is always at a grave disadvantage when any misunderstanding of his method or attitude arises. The most innocent things he has done in the best possible spirit are construed against him. To face things squarely, to state them frankly, and to insist always on complete publicity and entire freedom of discussion, is the only sound method of dealing with organizations of any kind."

All great characters have been conspicuous by their simplicity, their dependence upon great principles instead of secret policies. When Savonarola was bound on the rack to draw from him the schemes which his enemies declared he entertained, he said, "My secrets are few, because my purposes were great." There are no secret processes involved in great achievements.

Poets, painters, orators, and sculptors are often besought by curious souls to tell the secret of their achievements. They are asked concerning their great undertakings, again and again, "How did you do this?" The answer given by one of the greatest modern sculptors to a question of this kind is in point: A learned German professor who went to see Thorwaldsen in his studio, and was admiring one of his statues, began questioning him as to what course of study he had pursued. Thorwaldsen was at first puzzled, but said at last, "You want to know how I made this figure?" "Yes," said the professor, "I should like very much to know." "Well," said Thorwaldsen, speaking very slowly and distinctly, "I took a board and bored a hole in it, then I took a stick and put it to stand upright in the hole; after that I got a tub with wet clay and plastered it around the stick, and then — I shaped it." Perhaps the professor was not much wiser than before.

Carlyle emphasized the broad, free spirit in which all great things are fashioned and sustained in the phrase "the open secret" of the world. Not by scheming or underhanded plotting are we to grow in spiritual power, or to advance the cause of Christ, either in our own hearts or the world about us. The real "kingdom of God" must not be confused in our minds with what may be only its cast-off shell, from which the soul has long since fled. We have in our day the sad spectacle of a great spiritual detective headquarters in the Vatican in Rome, whose boast is that for shrewd diplomacy and intrigue in politics and religion it is unparalleled throughout the world, and yet claiming to be the centre of the Christian religion. We turn from such a sight ready to believe what Rev. Dr. J. W. Lee says in that brilliant book, "The Making of a Man": "Religion is not what men need to get these days. What the world is dying for and needing most of all is Christ. Religion is not a very good thing to have much of, unless it has been lifted and refined by contact with Christ. Many people have got too much religion; it weakens them and disqualifies them for thorough, honest work. It makes them indolent and conceited, and often in the way of people who want to do needed Christian work. Such people should throw away their old wheezing, self-contained, self-included religion, and get the Lord Christ, the Way, the Truth, and the Life, into their lives. Christ is truth, Christ is love, all summed up in the unity of a perfect, holy, divine life."

Dr. A. C. Dixon recalls the story that once an electric car stopped in Boston, and one of the passengers asked, "What is the matter?" "Oh," said the conductor, "nothing but dirt on the track." The dirt broke the current of power. Oftentimes all our sharpness and politic time-serving, instead of helping along, is only dirt on the track, hindering the work of God.

The clean, frank, open heart — that it is, that, shining in the countenance, speaking in our words, and living in simple deeds, will tell for truth. "John," said an artist the other day to a Chinaman, who was unwillingly acting as a model, "smile. If you don't look pleasant, I'll not pay you." "No use," grumbled the washerman. "If Chinaman feelee ugly all the time, he lookee ugly " — which is as true of every other man and woman in the world as of John Chinaman.

He whose heart is frankly open to Heaven's influence is like an artesian well ever sending forth living streams to bless the world. Faber expresses this thought beautifully when he says: "There are souls in the world who have the gift of finding joy everywhere, and of leaving it behind them when they go. Joy gushes from under their fingers like jets of life. Their influence is an inevitable gladdening of the heart. It seems as if a shadow of God's own gift had passed upon them. They give light without meaning to shine. These *bright hearts* have a great work to do for God."

And, finally, the result of this wise simplicity is that Satan's head is bruised.

In the darkest hour of trial, in the midst of the most disheartening circumstances, God has always stood by His people who lived with open hearts and loyal purpose. They have bruised Satan's head in his very stronghold, and sung songs of victory with their feet upon his lustful neck.

Dr. Wayland Hoyt tells how he was walking in one of the most squalid parts of London. The streets were long lines of low, blackened houses between which rolled the commonest traffic of the great town. It was bright summer day, but the sun could only partly pierce the overhanging canopy of smoke. There were countless children, unkempt and ill-clothed, whose school and playground were the verdureless and solid sidewalks. The homes they came out of were the meanest and meagerest. The whole aspect was that of a sickening desolateness; the whole place one of those sad blotches which greed and poverty and drink and dissoluteness gather and splash upon the fair, sweet order of God's world. Walking and musing thus, he was struck and startled by a bird's song — the strongest, cheeriest, soaring bird-note. He looked to see whence, amid such plight, the song could come, and saw in a small cage hanging by a poor window an imprisoned English skylark. The cage was small — just a few bits of wood nailed together — but within the cage there was a little patch of green sod, cut from some meadow. And amid the sod, with wings lifted as if for flight which would almost dare assault the sun, the brown bird was standing with head turned skyward, singing its heart out, raining melody upon all the noise, dust, and filth around.

So God gives His dearer singers "songs in the night." Paul and Silas shook down prison doors and struck off iron chains with midnight melodies, and Bunyan saw through the walls of a dungeon into unspeakable glories. O brothers, fear not. Live frankly, openly, purely, and your very frankness shall outwit the serpentine cunning of the adversary of souls. Your feet shall stand upon his head, and upon the head of all the spiritual enemies of your soul. Tennyson says, in his tribute to Christ in the dedication of "In Memoriam:" —

> "Thine are these orbs of light and shade;
>   Thou madest Life in man and brute;
>   Thou madest Death; and lo, Thy foot
> Is on the skull which Thou hast made.
>
> Thou wilt not leave us in the dust;
>   Thou madest man, he knows not why;
>   He thinks he was not made to die;
> And Thou hast made him: Thou art just.
>
> Thou seemest human and divine,
>   The highest, holiest manhood, Thou;
>   Our wills are ours, we know not how;
> Our wills are ours, to make them Thine."

And not only may we be cheered by promises of personal triumph, but we shall help on the victory of righteousness in the world. For Jesus Christ shall be King over all.

In one of his last poems, after contemplating the sins and sorrows of the world, Tennyson cries out triumphantly: —

> "Moaning your losses, O Earth,
>   Heart weary and overdone!
> But all's well that ends well,
>   Whirl, and follow the sun!
>
> He is racing from heaven to heaven,
>   And less will be lost than won,
> For all's well that ends well,
>   Whirl, and follow the sun!
>
> The reign of the Meek upon Earth,
>   O weary one, has it begun?
> But all's well that ends well,
>   Whirl, and follow the sun!
>
> For moans will have grown sphere-music,
>   Or ever your race be run!
> And all's well that ends well,
>   Whirl, and follow the sun!"

IV

THE SOUL'S RESOURCES

"In the meanwhile his disciples prayed him, saying, Master, eat. But he said unto them, I have meat to eat that ye know not of. Therefore said the disciples one to another, Hath any man brought him ought to eat? Jesus saith unto them, My meat is to do the will of him that sent me, and to finish his work." — JOHN iv. 31–34.

THE common tendency of life is toward extremes. On one hand a wild fanaticism; on the other, a sluggish, non-progressive conservatism. The silly chatter of empty giddiness holds one end of a line that rests its other end in the hand of the sour-faced, grumbling misanthrope. The bright-eyed optimist who sees triumph in every opening cycle keeps pace with the gloomy-browed pessimist who walks on coffins, and is sure that every century is hurling the nations and the race to final and irretrievable disaster. The text suggests a nice balance between two such extremes.

On one side is a starred independence, and on the other a childish and helpless dependence. The more common and more wretched soul is he who depends for every satisfaction on the whims, caprices, accidents, and vicissitudes of his own little social world. But it is given to us to possess some resources in ourselves, and entire dependence on others is a most dangerous habit of mind. The Master had meat to eat that even His faithful disciples knew not of; and all good men have such nourishment. To live our own life, to have meat in ourselves, is a privilege of immeasurable value: and such a life is enriched and made fruitful by the showers of divine grace, and is illuminated by the light of divine love.

I.

Our first thought, then, as we come to study this suggestive picture in the life of Jesus, is: *The Individuality of Life.*

Jesus came and walked His unheralded way of common life through the land of Palestine. Sometimes the multitudes thronged Him, and again He was alone among the mountains. One day they spread palm branches in His path and cried "Hosanna!" and on another they cried "Crucify him!" but whether it were praise or blame; whether the fickle tide of public feeling swayed toward Him as if to sweep Him onward to a throne, or surged backward to hang Him with thieves, He was the same self-possessed, patient, tender, forgiving, majestic character. He did not depend for success or peace of mind upon the multitude. There was an undercurrent in this noble life that none of the eddies and tides and storms of public frenzy could reach for a moment. His life went calmly on to its work whether men praised or cursed. He had meat to eat that they knew not of. And so all lives which are free from the slavery of sin and fashion and habit, may live an individual life that circumstances shall not control, but that rather shall control and make circumstances.

Emerson says, "Every true man is a cause, a country, and an age." A man Cæsar is born, and for years after we have a Roman Empire. Christ is born, and millions of minds so grow and cleave to His genius, that He is confounded with virtue and the possible man. An institution is the lengthened shadow of one man — monachism, of the hermit Anthony; the Reformation, of Luther; Quakerism, of Fox; Methodism, of Wesley; abolition, of Clarkson. Scipio, Milton called "the height of Rome;" and all history resolves itself very easily into the biography of a few stout, earnest persons. And what is true of these large souls which greatly impress the world with the power of their individuality might, in our own appropriate circle, be true of us all if we were not such miserable copyists. These great leading spirits have not worn out the virtues of life that made them great. And so marvellously has God arranged the balances of the universe that "as great stake may hang upon your private act of to-day as followed their public and renowned footsteps." There is more than one little ark of bulrushes at this moment holding its possible Moses, who may, however, settle down into a mere Egyptian dude, and eat and drink in the idleness and flabby uselessness of a fashionable career. How the world halts and stumbles because only one man or woman in a thousand is brave enough, and simple enough, to let the individuality of heart and mind and soul, with which God has endowed every new man and woman, have free play.

God is the one artist in the universe who needs never to repeat Himself in His pictures; and yet in how many circles do we make it seem as if He had done nothing else but repeat. Some frivolous, heartless Frenchwoman puts the body of a little bird upon her hat and goes strutting down the street in her borrowed plumage, and the women of a half-dozen nations cry aloud for the lives of the innocent songsters, until the forests threaten to be depopulated. And this is only an illustration of what goes on in literature and art and morals. We need a revival of individuality — a revival of that keen sense of personal worth and personal obligation which lies at the root of all deep earnestness.

This *proper valuation of our Individuality* becomes important when we reflect that all the great voices of the universe that are speaking to us with purpose, to enlighten, develop, and lift us up toward heaven, speak only to our individual being. These voices from the speaking earth and heavens, whether from nature or revelation, are indistinct or clear, tremulous or firm, full of meaning or void of meaning, according to the individual hearing of him who hears. One thus pictures our truth: —

"A group of men stands facing the same long sea line. The same voices of sea and shore are sounding in the ears of each individual of that group; yet the message which is borne to each is different. It may be that each message brings new impulses to him that hears it, but the impulses will be as diverse as the messages. One listener catches a note in the deep harmony of earth and sea, and reproduces it in a new piece of music; another embodies a revelation which came to him there in a poem; a third is impelled to transfer his vision of glory to the canvas; a fourth is drawn to a life of adventure on the ocean; and a fifth hears only the voice that tells him of a favorable opportunity for investment in shore-lands."

The poet tells us that,—

> "Along the shell-wreathed, shining strand
> The old and young went to and fro;
> The sinking sun filled all the land
> With evening's rich and ruddy glow.

The hot clouds in the amber west
   Lit up the sea-kissed, shingly bars,
And weary ones who longed for rest
   Waited the dawning of the stars.

There came the murmur of the sea
   Along the soft sands of the shore;
'Twas laden with deep mystery,
   And music strange was in its roar.
And, as the voices of the waves
   Were borne upon the listening ears,
They sang alike of songs and graves,
   Of sunny hearts and sacred tears.

There passed a little blue-eyed boy,
   As sank the sun on ocean's brim;
Naught but the sound of endless joy
   Across the red waves came to him.
For his bright fancy chased the sun
   O'er seas of emerald and gold;
And the sweet life he had begun
   Its first fair scenes had now unrolled.

With merry heart a maiden came
   The shining, sunlit sands along;
To her the sea bore one dear name
   Amid the burden of its song;
And the ten thousand glitterings
   That stretched across the sunlit bay
Seemed messengers on golden wings
   From her true loved one, far away.

There came a man of full fourscore
   Into the twilight all alone;

> To him the sea broke on the shore
>   With solemn sway and sullen moan.
> The voices of the bygone years
>   Came faintly on its sad refrain;
> Yet when he called, 'mid rising tears,
>   On friends, they answered not again.
>
> Still sank the sun. Then rose the stars,
>   And looked down on the cold, gray shore;
> Still solemnly the moaning bars
>   Wailed low their music as of yore.
> And some with sad eyes met the night,
>   To pass its watches all forlorn;
> And some there slept 'mid visions bright
>   Till dawned the fragrant, rosy morn."

Like that is the sea of life, of eternity. Like it is the sea of knowledge. These personal, individual souls will hear echoes after their kind.

A keen writer remarks that messages and impulses come to us from without, but they always come from something there that is akin to ourselves. The revelation to us of that which is wholly alien to us is impossible. Science has shown it to be probable that there are intense lights around us which the human eye cannot see, simply because the human eye has nothing within itself to answer to light undulations outside of a certain maximum and minimum range of length. Many people can hear the strident cry of bats; others, with keener ears in every other respect, can never hear that cry, simply because their own aural chords have no correspondence to sound waves of that particular dimension. Strike a note on the piano, and the corresponding string of the violin in the room becomes vibrant, while the other strings remain silent. A voice has spoken, and a kindred voice calls to it across the distance. So, —

> "There is in souls a sympathy with sounds;
> And as the mind is pitched the ear is pleased.
> With melting airs or martial, brisk or grave,
> Some chord in unison with what we hear
> Is touched within us and the heart replies."

Ah, look well to your individuality. The air is full of harmonies struck from the great heart of the Infinite, and we are to add our part to that music.

Our very existence here is a proof that in some way or other we have a special work to perform. Rev. Mark Guy Pearse relates that a piccolo player, thinking his instrument would not be missed among the crash of cymbals at a

Händel rehearsal, stopped playing. But Sir Michael Costa hushed the music of the whole orchestra, missing *him*. So God may be waiting and listening now for music which is in your heart, and within your power to awaken.

II.

Then we have another important thought suggested: *Each human soul is sent into the world on a special mission.* Jesus said, "My meat and drink is to do the will of him that *sent me.*" What nobility that thought adds to life! How it frees us from the narrow restraints and circumstances that hedge in other men. Jesus could not afford to be bound by the narrow restraints and limitations of Judea. He walked across their most sacred traditions and they snapped under His feet like cobwebs. He was a great Divine Messenger *sent to the world* to save it at infinite sacrifice. He could not afford to come down to the temporary joy of pleasing it. Such a consciousness brings a like freedom to men to-day, and ennobles all common life.

A poet tells the story of two singers: —

"One touched his futile lyre to please the ear
  And win the buzzing plaudits of the town ;
And sang a song that carolled loud and clear,
  And gained at once a blazing, brief renown.
Nor he, nor all that crowd behind him, saw
  The ephemeral list of pleasant rhymers dead —
Their verse once deemed a title without flaw
  To fame, whose phantom radiance long had fled.

Another sang his soul out to the stars
  And the deep hearts of men. The few who passed
Heard a low, thoughtful strain behind his bars,
  As of some captive in a prison cast;
And when that thrilling voice no more was heard,
  Him from his cell in funeral pomp they bore;
Then all that he had sung and written stirred
  The world's great heart with thoughts unknown before."

The man who feels that he is sent of God to accomplish an important mission is filled with the power of a great purpose. He who is the messenger of the King becomes deaf to the commands of all trivial persons. His soul is wrapped up in his mission.

A Russian officer was sent from Siberia to St. Petersburg in the dead of winter with messages of great importance to the Czar. He had to travel by sledge, and for many days and nights without rest and almost entirely without sleep. He hastened on his way till, worn and exhausted, he arrived at the palace, and was immediately taken to the Czar's presence. After giving his messages, the officer, standing as he was, dropped his head against the wall and was sound asleep. After a little time the Czar wished to ask him a question. Finding him asleep, he tried to waken him; he shouted and hallooed, but to no effect. Finally he went to him and repeated in his ear: "Your highness, the horses are now ready," and the man awakened with a start. Through all his long journey those words had been ringing in his ears at every station, and his soul had been possessed with the one thought of carrying his message swiftly through.

The power of one great purpose frees us from bondage to many of the smaller tyrants to which men and women who live aimless lives are subject.

Victor Hugo wrote his "Notre Dame" during the revolution of 1830, while bullets were whistling across his garden and barricades were being erected almost at his door. He shut himself up in one room, locking up his clothes lest they should tempt him to go out into the streets, and spent the whole of that winter wrapped up in a big gray comforter, pouring his whole soul into his work.

The noted literary lady, Mrs. Somerville, had the same power of becoming so absorbed in her work as to be unconscious of what was going on around her. Dr. Somerville, her husband, told Harriet Martineau that he once laid a wager with a friend that he would abuse Mrs. Somerville in a loud voice to her face, and that she would take no notice; and he did so. Sitting close to her, he confided to his friend the most injurious things — that she rouged, that she wore a wig, and other such nonsense, all uttered in a loud voice. Her daughters were in a roar of laughter, while the slandered lady sat placidly writing. At last her husband made a dead pause after her name, when she looked up innocently, and said, "Did you speak to me?"

So if you will fill my heart and soul with the conviction that my life is dear to God, that He has made me in His own image and likeness in order that I might do some of His work in the universe; that I am not here somehow or other, by some strange freak or accident, but that the infinite wisdom of the Almighty and Eternal God has sent me here for a special purpose and to do work of great moment ; get me to believe that with all my heart, and how free and brave and strong do you make me ! I know some people profess to believe that, and still live on shrinking, cowardly, indifferent lives — lives no higher or braver than the dog in his kennel, or the ox in his stall. But no man or woman ever yet really believed that without being filled with a strange exaltation. And such a consciousness is possible for us all.

On the walls of the National Gallery in London hangs one of the greatest paintings of Sir Joshua Reynolds. It is "The Infant Samuel." The picture tells the old familiar Bible story. It represents Samuel on that night in the temple when the Lord called him to that special work for which he was designed. He is represented just as he really was — a child suddenly aroused from sleep, bewildered by a voice that calls him, and simply and confidingly responding to the direction of his aged guardian and friend to answer the voice. The upraised, astonished, yet trustful, young face is before us while we almost hear the half-parted, childish lips as they utter the words, " Speak, Lord; for thy servant heareth."

Perhaps some of you are saying to yourselves that if God would come to you with a vision like that — so distinct and plainly marked — and point out your especial work, you would be able to enter upon it with assurance and with gladness. And yet has not God called you as distinctly as He did Samuel? There may not in your case have been the same old Jewish temple, the dark midnight, the audible voice; but these were only the accidents which surrounded this case. The call, equally as direct and impressive, might under other circumstances have come to him in his mother's dooryard at home.

In some way, each in His own way, God calls each of us that he may *send* us to our work. Open the ear, my brother, to the heavenly call!

And there is this sublime comfort further to be remembered — that if we are conscious of being sent of God to our work, then we know our work itself must finally come to victory. If I am doing my own work, I have no reason to believe that it will last longer than the feeble hands that build; but if it is God's work, and He has sent me to do it, I know that not one stroke of my feeble hammer shall fall unnoticed, or fall with empty echo down the halls of the ages; and though I, and those who come after me for generations, may be gathered home before the temple of liberty and truth and perfect manhood shall reach its top-stone, I know that top-stone shall be raised amid the shouts of a ransomed and redeemed universe.

There is a beautiful legend of Walter von der Vogelweid, one of the principal minnesingers of the thirteenth century, how that, feeling his end to be near, he left all his treasures to the chapter of the Würzburg Cathedral, on the condition that the birds might be fed daily at noontide on his place of rest. And the legend tells how they were feasted every noon by the children of the choir, and how that, as time went on, the glad news was spread athwart the blue heavens in melodious joy from thousands of feathered throats, till to that tomb which was scattered over with grain as with the benison of life,—
"Day by day in vaster numbers
Flocked the poets of the air."

Time with gnawing tooth has long ago effaced from his tombstone the name of Vogelweid, and the spot where his bones lie no one knows; but still the projecting eaves of Würzburg's minster towers echo the twitter of the pilgrim swallow, its heart laden perchance with memories of Damascus or Carmel. The pious, grateful minnesinger who left such a sweet, provident legacy to his winged, melodious teachers now sleeps in the silence of oblivion, —

> "But around the vast cathedral,
> By sweet echoes multiplied,
> Still the birds repeat the legend
> And the name of Vogelweid."

So God has made many a good man's grave to be scattered with food for those that came after him, and made the honest work of his long-ago-dead hands to re-echo in music of joy centuries after he has disappeared from the walks of men.

III.

And then our text is full of a great concluding thought. We have suggested here *the proper food of the soul.*

Jesus says, "My meat is to do the will of

him that sent me." If Jesus had depended for spiritual food on the human appreciation of the men He served, what a poor, beggared, starved life would have been His. But was ever life so full and rich in spiritual abundance as the life of Jesus? His patience, charity, and forgiving love never gave out; and the reason was in the fact that His food was received from a heavenly source. He had "meat to eat" that they knew not of. Christ's hidden meat was to do the will of the Father. Obedience fed Him. Fidelity refreshed His soul, and pure conduct made Him strong. If we are to do Christlike work among men, we must be fed with the same kind of meat,—obedience to God, fidelity to Him and His work, and purity of life. If we have such food, our souls will not famish merely because human honor or earthly rewards are denied to us. He who sits down with Jesus to such a banquet need not sorrow because the world has neglected to invite him to its feasts of pride. How indescribably precious is this truth! We may have a perpetual feast with the Master at the head of the table. In all the poverty of worldly resources that may threaten us with annoyance, we may draw without stint or limit upon the eternal treasury.

Dr. Arthur Edwards, in an editorial of great power in the *Northwestern Christian Advocate* some years since, says: "It is an awful thing to despise such an opportunity, and prefer the husks of pride to the bounties of eternal goodness. Even the prodigal son found a bad taste in the husks; all sinners, sooner or later, come to that bitter experience. There is only one abiding joy for men, and that is Christ's joy, the joy of doing the will of God. There must be an evil spirit within us when we turn away from this satisfaction and try once more, as millions have done before us, to gnaw some nourishment from the bones of vanity. There is a divine life in us, when we can, like the Master, nourish our joys on the purposes which drive us forward in the paths of obedience. Is it not worth while to ask on what do we feed our souls? Let us ask ourselves the sources of the pleasures of the spirit. Let us take an inventory of our delights. Have we any which come from well-doing? Then we have a common bond with the Master. His wealth was all of this sort; He had no other; and yet He was the richest soul in the fellowship of the race. You never tried His way of happiness sincerely without satisfaction; and no other way has ever pleased or profited you long at a time. All the experiences of men which run parallel with that of Jesus are happy experiences. All others run down inevitably into decay and death. The years become too numerous. The delights of the flesh pall on the palate; and strength succumbs to disease and death. This outward life is only a show of life — galvanized, as it were, into a spasmodic imitation of life, and relapsing into death when the strange, concealed battery ceases to play upon the quivering flesh. It is a fire in a stove which must always be replenishing, and which no replenishing will keep burning very long."

It is only the soul that truly lives, and may be fed with self-feeding forces. O brothers, sisters! shall we not learn the secret of our blessed Master's self-centred and self-springing joy? Shall we not — as He — learn to live on duties done, crosses borne, hopes resigned, and sorrows welcomed as the very angels of God?

Now, and ever, it is true that only in that submission that can say, "Thy will be done," is there perfect nourishment and rest for a human soul. Helen Hunt Jackson learned this lesson, and sings it to us in sweet and helpful lay, —

" Blindfolded and alone I stand,
With unknown thresholds on each hand ;
　The darkness deepens as I grope,
　Afraid to fear, afraid to hope ;
Yet this one thing I learn to know
Each day more surely as I go :
　That doors are opened, ways are made,
　Burdens are lifted or are laid,
By some great law unseen and still.
Unfathomed purpose to fulfil,
　　Not as I will.

Blindfolded and alone I wait ;
Loss seems too bitter, gain too late ;
　Too heavy burdens in the load,
　And too few helpers on the road ;
And joy is weak, and grief is strong,
And years and days so long, so long.
　Yet this one thing I learn to know
　Each day more surely as I go :
That I am glad the good or ill
By changeless law are ordered still,
　　Not as I will.

' Not as I will!' The sound grows sweet
Each time my lips the words repeat ;

> 'Not as I will;' the darkness feels
> More safe than light when this thought steals
> Like whispered voice to calm and bless
> All unrest and all loneliness.
> 'Not as I will,' because the One
> Who loved us first and best is gone
> Before us on the road, and still
> For us must all His love fulfil,
>   Not as we will."

One of the prettiest conceits in those quaint books given us by "Uncle Remus" is put into the mouth of an old negro driver. He ran away from his old master, and could not be caught; but an old lady bought him because he had saved the life of her son, and he surrendered himself and became a faithful servant. When his old mistress came to die, her wandering mind dwelt upon the negro who had served her so faithfully. She fancied she was making a journey. "The carriage goes smoothly along here," she murmured. Then, after a little pause, she asked, "Is David driving?" And the weeping negro from the corner of the room cried, "'Tain't po' Dave, Mistis! De good Lord done took holt er de lines." And so, dreaming as a child would dream, the old lady slipped from life into the better land. Dear brethren, the path will never seem so smooth, our chariot of destiny will never glide so swiftly toward its heavenly mansion, as when the Lord has taken the lines of our lives into His own hand. Shall we not gladly yield them to such keeping even in this hour?

V

AN EARNEST LIFE

"Whatsoever thy hand findeth to do, do it with thy might; for there is no work, nor device, nor knowledge, nor wisdom, in the grave, whither thou goest." — ECCL. ix. 10.

THE present age is largely in sympathy with this text. There is little charity shown for drones or sluggards, either in things temporal or spiritual. We are impatient of delay. The days of travel by stage-coach and sailing-vessels are soon to be forgotten. We are not willing to wait even for fast steamers to carry our news across the great waters. We tie the continents together with our iron cables, and send our lightning-winged messages under the sea, until we laugh at distance and space. The great channels of intercommunication are whetting the nations against each other until the sparks fly. It is an age of white heat. He who keeps pace with the world to-day does not want to be napping by the way. He who wins must be in earnest, and look well to his gait, or he will be left behind. A popular author says, "The secret of all worldly success is earnestness."

My purpose is much broader and higher than to talk to you simply of worldly success. I come to speak to you as candidates for immortality, whose main interests lie in the vast future, who shall live when time is dead, and may shine when yonder sun is quenched. And as the work devolving upon us is so momentous, and the time allotted to us so short, I do not know of a passage in all the Bible better suited for our study than this that I have read. What we are to do must soon be accomplished. We are here to do things. And nothing but the active work which is appointed to us can fill up the measure of our destiny.

At a gathering of Socialists at Geneva, Switzerland, quite a dramatic close of a session of the so-called reformers was brought about by a suggestive incident. The speakers talked much of the real and fancied wrongs of the poor and the workingmen; but when in the midst of his graceful periods a well-dressed dandy was asked by a brawny, grimy mechanic to show his hands, there arose a great uproar, and the meeting broke up in confusion.

And so we are hastening on to the time, dear brethren, when the earnest Carpenter from Nazareth — He of the nail-wounded palm — will demand of us all to show our hands for the signs of Christian toil. God grant that we may not be put to confusion by such a demand.

Let us study, then, —

THE ELEMENTS OF AN EARNEST LIFE.

First of all we may say with assurance that an earnest life is the outgrowth of an earnest faith. The doubter is never in earnest. The man who only half believes his cause is right gives to it only faint-hearted service. The volcano is the outward manifestation of the hidden fire. Down deep in the earth it burns through the ages, until its energy can no longer be contained, and then it bursts its bounds in terrific explosions that shake the continent and tear the mountains asunder. So an earnest life is the outward manifestation of a hidden fire in the soul. A man becomes convinced of a great truth. A live, important, earnest faith takes possession of his being, becomes his master; and henceforth he is its obedient servant. You see this illustrated in the representative of every great reformation. William Lloyd Garrison once, when his friends complained that he was too earnest, declared: " I am convinced that human slavery is wrong and only wrong. I will be as harsh as truth, and as uncompromising as justice. On this subject I do not wish to think or speak or write with moderation. Go tell a man whose house is on fire to give a moderate alarm! Tell a mother moderately to rescue her babe from the flames where it has fallen! But do not urge me to use moderation in a cause like the present. I am in earnest — I will not equivocate; I will not excuse; I will not retreat a single inch; and I will be heard. The apathy of the people is enough to make every statue of liberty leap from its pedestal, and to hasten the resurrection from the dead." There was earnestness for you; and is it not easy to see that it was the outflow of a deep, earnest faith which had taken possession of the man's soul?

The poet says, —

"Count me o'er earth's chosen heroes; they were souls that stood alone
While the men they agonized for hurled the contumelious stone;
Stood serene, and down the future saw the golden beam incline
To the side of perfect justice, mastered by their faith divine,
By one man's plain truth to manhood and to God's supreme design.

By the light of burning heretics Christ's bleeding feet I track
Toiling up new Calvaries ever with the cross that turns not back.
And these mounts of anguish number how each generation learned
One new word of that grand Credo which in prophet-hearts hath burned
Since the first man stood God-conquered with his face to heaven upturned.

For humanity sweeps onward; where to-day the martyr stands,
On the morrow crouches Judas, with the silver in his hands;
Far in front the cross stands ready, and the crackling fagots burn,
While the hooting mob of yesterday in silent awe return
To glean up the scattered ashes for history's golden urn."

It is the earnest faith that gives the prophet eye, and the iron will that makes a man master of himself. It is related of Marshal Ney that once on going into battle he noticed that his knees were smiting together from fear. Looking down at them, he said: "You may well shake. You'd shake worse yet if you knew where I am going to take you." That was Ney holding Ney to the line of duty in spite of the terror that curdled the blood; and it was that self-mastery that gave him the reputation of "the bravest of the brave." So when our lives grow sluggish we may know that faith is losing its earnestness. Go to the fountain of faith! Refresh the purpose at the feet of the Great Teacher, and the life will blossom with earnestness and power.

Coupled with an earnest faith there must be an earnest love; otherwise the life, however earnest, may grow hard and narrow. There is nothing like an earnest love to feed the rootlets of a life. It sweetens the bitterest cup of human toil. It makes self-sacrifice a joy. And nothing else has such a magical power over men around us as the conviction that we love them.

There is a quaint, sweet story of a Scotch potter who had one small invalid child at home. He wrought at his trade with great fidelity, being always on hand at the opening hour. He managed to bear each evening to the bedside of the "wee lad," as he called him, a flower or a bit of ribbon, a fragment of crimson glass — indeed, anything that would lie out on the white counterpane and give a color in the room. He was a quiet, unsentimental Scotchman, but he never went home at nightfall without some toy or trinket, showing that he had remembered the wan face that lit up so when he came in. I presume he never said to a living soul that he loved that sick child so much; still, he went on patiently loving him. And by and by he moved that whole shop into a positively real but unconscious fellowship with him. The workmen made curious jars and teacups on their wheels, and painted diminutive pictures down the sides before they stuck them in corners of the kiln at burning-time. One brought some fruit in the bulge of his apron, and another some engravings in a rude scrap-book. Not one of them all said a word, for this solemn thing was not talked about. They put them in the old man's hat, where he found them and understood all about it. And that entire pottery full of men grew more quiet and kind as the months drifted. And some of the ungoverned ones stopped swearing as they noticed the weary look on the old Scotchman's face, and knew that the inevitable shadow was drawing nearer. Every day somebody did a piece of his work as the little lad grew worse, so that he could come later and go earlier. So one day when the bell tolled, and the little coffin came out of the door of the lowly house, there stood a hundred stalwart workingmen from the pottery, with their clean clothes, most of whom gave a half-day of time for the privilege of taking off their hats to that simple procession, filing in behind it, and following across the village green to its grave that small burden of a child which probably not one had ever seen with his own eyes.

Such is the power of love. An earnest love is a fountain from which flows an earnest life. If you wonder sometimes why you are so lacking in earnestness in trying to save men, study your own heart, and see if it is not a lack of love for them. Those we love we are earnest enough about, and love is the key that will unlock the heart that shows only a wall of iron to any other touch.

But an earnest life must have a worthy object. The very conception of an earnest life along the line I have indicated is that of a life supremely devoted to God; a life that feels keenly its personal responsibility; a soul that realizes its own inherent grandeur, and therefore the grandeur of every other human soul. We can express this devotion to God in two ways — by the purity of our own personal character, and by helping others about us. So no soul can fail to manifest its devotion. We may be so hemmed in by our circumstances that we are helpless to do any outward act for God; but none are so helpless but that by God's grace they can be pure and good, and thus serve Him by being something if not by doing something. And sometimes to these silent lives of unstained purity God gives voices of great power in making the bad world better.

Whatever we do with a sincere and honest purpose for our fellow-men as unto the Lord,

He regards as done for Himself. The Saviour's description in Matthew's record of the scenes of the final reckoning is most comforting. "Then," said Jesus, "shall the King say unto them on his right hand, Come, ye blessed of my Father, inherit the kingdom prepared for you from the foundation of the world: For I was an hungred, and ye gave me meat: I was thirsty, and ye gave me drink: I was a stranger, and ye took me in: naked, and ye clothed me: I was sick, and ye visited me: I was in prison, and ye came unto me. Then shall the righteous answer him, saying, Lord, when saw we thee an hungred, and fed thee? or thirsty, and gave thee drink? When saw we thee a stranger, and took thee in? or naked, and clothed thee? Or when saw we thee sick, or in prison, and came unto thee? And the King shall answer and say unto them, . . . Inasmuch as ye have done it unto one of the least of these my brethren, ye have done it unto me."

Lowell, in his poem recounting his story of Sir Launfal, beautifully pictures this truth. When the knight was young, he started out on a pilgrimage in search of the Holy Grail. As he started out he met a poor leper, but bent on his misguided quest he flung his alms to the beggar in contempt; but as he comes back, worn with the struggle of life and sweetened by affliction and failure, he meets again a leper, and with tender heart shares with him his crust of bread, feeling that it is a service for Christ. Lowell says. —

> "Sir Launfal sees only the grewsome thing,
> The leper, lank as the rain-blanched bone,
> That cowers beside him, a thing as lone
> And white as the ice-isles of Northern seas
> In the desolate horror of his disease.
>
> And Sir Launfal said, 'I behold in thee
> An image of him who died on the tree;
> . . . .
> Mild Mary's Son, acknowledge me;
> Behold, through him I give to thee.'
>
> Then the soul of the leper stood up in his eyes
> And looked at Sir Launfal, and straightway he
> Remembered in what a haughtier guise
> He had flung an alms to leprosie,
> When he girt his young life up in gilded mail
> And set forth in search of the Holy Grail.
> The heart within him was ashes and dust;
> He parted in twain his single crust,
> He broke the ice on the streamlet's brink,
> And gave the leper to eat and drink.
> 'Twas a mouldy crust of coarse brown bread,
> 'Twas water out of a wooden bowl; —

Yet with fine wheaten bread was the leper fed,
And 'twas red wine he drank with his thirsty soul.

As Sir Launfal mused with a downcast face,
A light shone round about the place;
The leper no longer crouched at his side,
But stood before him glorified,
Shining and tall and fair and straight
As the pillar that stood by the Beautiful Gate, —
Himself the Gate whereby men can
Enter the temple of God in man.

His words were shed softer than leaves from the pine,
And they fell on Sir Launfal as snow on the brine,
That mingle their softness and quiet in one
With the shaggy unrest they float down upon;
And the voice that was softer than silence said,
' Lo, it is I, be not afraid!
In many climes, without avail,
Thou hast spent thy life for the Holy Grail;
Behold, it is here, — this cup which thou
Didst fill at the streamlet for me but now;
This crust is my body broken for thee,
This water his blood that died on the tree;
The Holy Supper is kept, indeed,
In whatso we share with another's need;
Not what we give, but what we share,
For the gift without the giver is bare;
Who gives himself with his alms feeds three,
Himself, his hungering neighbor, and me."

The support of an earnest life must be, first and last, reliance upon God. God is its origin and its strength. No man can lead such a life without knowing that he stands not alone; that an almighty Arm is stretched out for his support. Cæsar once said to a ferryman who was fearful of wreck in a storm, "Fear not, thou carriest Cæsar and his fortunes." So the really earnest soul is borne up with the conviction that he cannot fail, since he carries the destiny of truth, the fortunes of God. No man has a solid foundation on which to build an earnest life who does not have an almighty faith in the immortality of truth, the ultimate triumph of every right over every wrong. The old German poet, Von Logau, more than two hundred years ago said,

> " The mills of God grind slowly,
> But they grind exceeding small
> Though with patience He stands waiting,
> With exactness He grinds all "

How they grind, those solemn mills of God! The glacier is one. In its snail like but tireless flow, it grinds from the primitive rocks that which will by and by be soil. The rain and the snow are mills of God. Through them not only is life supported on the earth, but from the mountain-sides the earth and the rock are washed away to make fertile the valleys. The sunlight is still another. Through its noiseless grinding the earth and the air grow warm, flowers spring up, and harvest fields grow golden. The rivers are the mills of God. As they grind their way they become the arteries through which the life of cities and nations is sustained. The ocean is the mightiest mill of all. But for its steady grinding all life would cease on the earth; the earth itself would become but the corpse of a world. These mills have been forever grinding, since through the first one the gases which floated in space were drawn, and this planet was rounded into form. These solemn mills of God are grinding away the earth. When thirsty, we drink a glass of water, and bless the fountains which feed the stream upon the mountain side. The real fountain is probably the Indian Ocean, and the cup of water of which we drink perhaps made a part of the water in which whales were playing two years ago, off the coast of Asia. In an elevator in one of the mills of God it was picked up from the hot seas; the trade winds, which are part of the motive power of those mills, bore it northward; as the earth revolved, the wind which blew straight was made to seem to bend to the east; the cloud, a hopper of the mill, which received it from the elevator, was carried over the Cascade Mountains. In the cool chambers of the air the cloud was concentrated, and the moisture fell upon the mountains in purest snow. Under the grinding of the summer sun the snow turned to water; the fissures of the immemorial rocks opened their gates to receive it; from them it found its way to the surface lower down; and these made the source of the creek or river from which our thirst was quenched. So these mills grind out their mercies perpetually, and man accepts them, sometimes gratefully and sometimes indifferently. But the mills grind on.

The mills of God have been grinding on human hearts for, lo! these sixty recorded centuries; and though it is the hardest work they ever tried, still they grind on, grinding out the base ores, and treasuring up the gold. Whole races rise up as tyrants and oppressors, and place their foot of power on the neck of the weaker races, and declare that serfdom, not freedom, shall be the law of life. Men hunt their brothers with bloodhounds, and tear Bibles to pieces to make poultices for the lacerated consciences; but all the time the solemn mills of God keep their crushers and shaking tables running, until they grind out slavery and grind in the liberty of man. And so to-day the mills are grinding, and the quartz, the mixed rock and earth and gold in principle and life, is being tossed into the hopper by brawny hands.

There goes in much of wrong and sin. I look abroad, and I see states and nations that " frame mischief by a law." I see governments that give to one man power to put that to his neighbor's lips which makes him a slave. I see multitudes reeling, staggering, falling to their death under a legalized system of murder. I see a world thronging with paupers and beggars, who are the victims of a legalized system of robbery. I hear the sighing and moaning of millions of the broken-hearted, that break on the ear like the sad wail of the angry, storm-beaten sea, whose hearts are broken under a legalized system of cruelty; and yet I hear Christian men standing even inside the pulpit of God's house to utter their doubts as to whether it will ever be overturned. Ah, sir, no man who does not trust God more than that will ever be an earnest worker for the uplifting of humanity. If you are ever tempted to doubt, go out in the stillness of the night and listen, as you scan the world of stars, to the grinding of those grand old mills of God, between whose mighty burrs all wrong shall be ground to powder, and only gold be saved. In the atmosphere of such a confidence only can a man enter upon a career of divine earnestness to which God is calling all of us.

And then, in conclusion, let us listen to the motives for an earnest life. We have only to listen to the text, "For there is no work, nor device, nor knowledge, nor wisdom, in the grave, whither thou goest." No time to be lost; no trifling with life's work, for the grave is at hand; what we are to do must be done now or never. A soldier condemned to die once crowded himself into the presence of Frederick the Great, with an order for a pardon in his hands, and said, "Sire, can I have one word with you?" "Yes," said the testy monarch, "one word, and if you utter more than one you lose your head." The soldier, possessed by the great earnestness of his desire for life, thrust the paper before the king's face and shouted, "Sign!" So our time is so brief, it is necessary for us to train ourselves down to action, find out what there is for us to do, and do it with our might. In this short, school-day period of existence we are training a life which is to outlast the ages.

Among the Hartz Mountains in Germany, there is a spot up to which tourists are often asked to walk in the after part of the day, in order that they may see what is called the Spectre of the Brocken. A vast reach of hills appears terraced away into the distance, across whose blue expanse a great figure in human shape is seen moving. Now, it requires some little attention before one can discover that this phenomenon is only his own shadow projected by the sun behind his back. That brow, whose nod seems as if it might shake the universe, is simply his own forehead; that hand, which might grapple with the Titans, is only his own with the staff in it that he climbed up by.

Here is a picture for our study. This character being formed now is to be projected forward upon the mountains of the unexplored eternity. Even at this moment it begins to exhibit the vastness of its future. It is not this arm you are waving, but that of yonder giant; it is not this foot you are leading onward, but that of the giant. It is not this life at all, but that other life, wherein lies the majesty, and wherein centres the hope of your entire being.

Then let me close as I began, " Whatsoever thy hand findeth to do, do it with thy might: for there is no work, nor device, nor knowledge, nor wisdom, in the grave, whither thou goest."

VI

ANXIETY, ITS DANGER AND ITS CURE

"In nothing be anxious; but in everything by prayer and supplication with thanksgiving let your requests be made known unto God." — Phil. iv. 6 (R. V.).

ANXIETY is a wholesale trouble-maker. It demoralizes its victim, and robs him of his wonted power in the wise ordering of his life. The wholesome, quiet mind, with all its resources at command, is needed in the successful performance of the duties which constantly confront us on the voyage of life. The sea-captain, after his vessel has passed out of sight of land, depends upon his chronometer and his compass. If these instruments fail him, then everything fails. And what the chronometer and compass are to the master of a ship, the sensitive and loyal fidelity of the powers of the human mind is to the success of our life voyage. Anything that unbalances the judgment and causes a panic in the brain, may cause the wreck of all our hopes.

I do not mean, and the Scripture does not teach, that we are not to wisely prepare for the duties and dangers of to-morrow. As has been said: "To foresee trouble and get ready for it is not to borrow trouble. The foreseen trouble actually comes to us; the borrowed trouble is unnecessarily added. At this moment, when so many are unable to borrow money on what would ordinarily be good security, every man finds himself able to borrow trouble without putting up any collateral. Trouble is to be had in every market, and every man can take as much as he chooses. The more he borrows, however, the less likely will he be able to successfully deal with what actually comes to him. It is a fact of experience which we are slow to learn, that the trouble we borrow never would have been ours in any other way. We appropriate what would never come to us otherwise. The real troubles of life are numerous and hard enough, but they constitute a very small proportion of its trials in comparison with imaginary troubles. To deal successfully with the real troubles, we must refuse to consider the imaginary ones."

Henry Ward Beecher once drew a vivid picture of how unholy passions sometimes work upon the soul as a mighty tempest beats upon the ocean and lashes it into wild fury: "Fear sits in the window. 'What seest thou?' says Vanity. 'Whisperings are abroad,' says Fear. 'Men are pointing at you — or they will as soon as you come to a point of observation.' 'Oh, my good name!' says the man. 'All that I have done; all that I have laid up — what will become of that? Where is my reputation going? What will become of me when I lose it, and when folks turn away from me? O trouble! trouble! it is coming!' What is it? Fear is sitting in the window of the soul, and looking into the future, and interpreting the signs thereof to the love of approbation in its coarsest and lowest condition.

"Fear still sits looking into the future, and Pride, coming up, says, 'What is it you see?' 'I see,' says Fear, 'your castle robbed. I see you topple down from your eminence. I see you under base men's feet. I see you weakened. I see you disgraced. I see your power scattered and gone.' 'O Lord! what a world this is!' says Pride. Now, that man has not had a particle of trouble. Fear sat at the window and lied. And Pride cried, and Vanity cried, and Avarice cried — and ought to cry. Fear sat and told lies to them all. Fear has a kaleidoscope which is full of broken glass, and it gives false pictures continually."

If you are to live a life full of usefulness and beneficence, you must not look at the universe through the lens of your fears. For fear is always seeing wrong. But every man or woman who takes hold of life with courageous vigor, and lives it in unswerving faith, not only insures " peace which passeth all understanding " to their own souls, but makes life richer and larger to countless thousands of their weaker fellows in life's battles.

But how may I cure this disposition toward anxiety which is within me? First of all, by reminding myself of the divine good-will toward me. God is, and is a rewarder of those who faithfully serve Him. The darkness turns to light, and the anxiety to confidence, when we grasp the conception of God's personal care for us.

A missionary among the Indians relates this incident. Some years ago an Indian stood at his door, and, as he opened the door, knelt at his feet. Of course he bade him not kneel. But the Indian said, "My father, I only knelt because my heart is warm to a man that pities the red man. I am a wild man. My home is five hundred miles from here. I knew that all the Indians east of the Mississippi had perished, and I never looked into the faces of my dear children that my heart was not sad. My father had told me of the Great Spirit, and I have often gone out into the woods and tried to talk to Him." Then he said, so sadly, as he looked in the minister's face, "You don't know what I mean. You never stood in the dark and reached out your hand and could not take hold of anything. And I heard one say that you had brought to the red man a wonderful story of the Son of the Great Spirit." That man sat as a child, and he heard anew the story of the love of Jesus. When they met again he looked in his friend's face and said, as he laid his hand on his heart, "It is not dark: it laughs all the while."

And my heart cannot help laughing, my brother, when I feel that, —

"The winds that o'er my ocean run
Reach through all worlds, beyond the sun, —
Through life, through death, through fate, through time,
Grand breaths of God, they sweep sublime.

Eternal trades, they cannot veer,
And, blowing, teach us how to steer;
And well for him whose joy, whose care,
Is but to keep before them fair.

O thou God's mariner, heart of mine,
Spread canvas to the airs divine!
Spread sail! and let thy fortune be
Forgotten in thy destiny.

A thread of law runs through thy prayer,
Stronger than iron cables are;
And love and longing toward her goal
Are pilots sweet to guide the soul."

Our anxiety and unrest are often born of the close, smothering atmosphere into which we try to crowd our souls — thus shutting out the presence of God. Professor Drummond grandly says, "The soul, in its highest sense, is a vast capacity for God. It is like a curious chamber added on to being, — a chamber with elastic and contractile walls, which can be expanded, with God as its guest, illimitably; but which, without God, shrinks and shrivels until every vestige of the divine is gone, and God's image is left without God's spirit. Nature has her revenge upon neglect as well as upon extravagance. Misuse, with her, is as mortal a sin as abuse."

But when we open our hearts to God everything changes. Our attitude to the whole universe changes. We are no longer orphaned and alone; we are in our Father's house. All teaching, all material things, all human activities, all present experience, all future experience — all, all are ours. Why? How do they become ours? Paul tells us why. Because we are Christ's, and Christ is God's. They are ours because they belong to Christ, and we belong to Christ. They are Christ's because Christ belongs to God, and all things belong to God. The house belongs to the children because it belongs to the Father.

Dr. Lyman Abbott graphically sets forth this trusteeship, which is held for our good in every power that touches our lives: You go into a hospital; here are the wards, here the beds, here the medicines, here the surgical apparatus; and it all belongs to the medical faculty, but for a purpose: it is theirs because put in their hands in trust to work out the cure of their patients. They are not to say, These are poisons; they are dangerous: we must put them away; we must not use them. They must learn the danger, and what is the wrong way and what the right way to use the poisons, and use them for the purpose for which they are given.

You go on board a great ocean steamer, and the moment the steamer leaves her dock you are under the absolute control of the captain; he is an autocrat, so far as the crew and passengers are concerned: the whole steamer belongs to him. He can shut you in your room, he can put you in irons, and there is no revolt possible. Why is it his? It is his that he may carry you safely across the ocean. If he uses this power that is put into his hands for himself and his own benefit, then he is recreant. When the Oregon, coming along the Atlantic coast, was struck in the middle of the night by that coaster, and a great wound was made in her side, through which the water was pouring, Captain Murray stood on the bridge as calm, apparently, as a May morning, and waited until every passenger was off, and every officer was off, and every man in the crew was off, and the last man to step from the sinking ship was the captain himself; and ten minutes after he stepped off, the steamer gave a quiver, as of apprehension, and then plunged to the bottom of the ocean. The steamer was his, and the men were his, and the boats were his, and the passengers were his, all for this: that he might save them in time of peril; and he should go down to the bottom of the ocean rather than that, by his recreancy, one of those intrusted to him should perish. That is the reason why all things are yours and mine — because we are Christ's, and Christ is God's. He says, " I am the good Shepherd, and know my sheep, . . . and I lay down my life for the sheep."

Oh, that we may catch the spirit of Paul's triumphant words! If we do, we shall be able to live in the atmosphere of Peter's injunction —

"casting all your care upon him, for he careth for you." Some poet, studying these words, has breathed a song which may help us all, —

> "What can it mean? Is it aught to Him
> That the nights are long and the days are dim?
> Can He be touched by the griefs I bear,
> Which sadden the heart and whiten the hair?
> Around His throne are eternal calms,
> And strong, glad music of happy psalms,
> And bliss unruffled by any strife —
> How can He care for my poor life?
>
> And yet I want Him to care for me,
> While I live in this world where the sorrows be.
> When the lights die down on the path I take;
> When strength is feeble and friends forsake;
> When love and music, that once did bless,
> Have left me to silence and loneliness;
> And life-song changes to sobbing prayers —
> Then my heart cries out for a God who cares.
>
> When shadows hang o'er me the whole day long,
> And my spirit is bowed with shame and wrong;
> When I am not good, and the deeper shade
> Of conscious sin makes my heart afraid;
> And the busy world has too much to do
> To stay in its course to help me through;
> And I long for a Saviour — can it be
> That the God of the universe cares for me?
>
> Oh, wonderful story of deathless love!
> Each child is dear to that Heart above.

> He fights for me when I cannot fight;
> He comforts me in the gloom of night;
> He lifts the burden, for He is strong;
> He stills the sigh and awakens the song;
> The sorrow that bowed me down He bears,
> And loves and pardons, because He cares.
>
> Let all who are sad take heart again,
> We are not alone in our hours of pain;
> Our Father stoops from His throne above
> To soothe and quiet us with His love.
> He leaves us not when the storm is high,
> And we have safety, for He is nigh.
> Can it be trouble which He doth share?
> Oh, rest in peace, for the Lord *does* care."

We shall be able to come to this assurance of God's interest in us and personal love for us by communion with Him. Listen to the injunction of the text, "In everything by prayer and supplication with thanksgiving let your requests be made known unto God."

A sainted mother, who lived to an old age, spoke often of the "mount of vision." When she was a young mother she had all her own housework to do, and a large family made constant demands upon her time and strength. "I had so much work in the valley," she would say, "that if it had not been for the 'mount of vision,' I could not have possessed my soul in patience. When I became impatient, and inclined to be what many of us call nervous, ready to speak quick words and pass unjust judgment, I would go alone into my bedroom, and, shutting the door, tell it to Jesus. That room was my 'mount of vision;' for I always saw with a clearer light my weakness, and received strength from the Lord to administer my government in the home with equity and more of a Christlike spirit."

Not only in home affairs, but in the gravest matters of statesmanship and the most trying turmoil of business cares, God has met His saints, relieved their anxiety, and given them peace and power.

Nehemiah went before the Persian king in regard to the broken walls of Jerusalem, after days and nights of prayer; and God gave him such resources of argument and such pathos of appeal that every obstacle melted before him. Job talked with God in the midst of a business panic that seemed hopeless; and peace and composure and prosperity came back to him.

Nothing can give us over to anxiety if we

keep close in touch with God. The future, as well as the past, we can safely trust to Him. In life or in death we may confidently sing, with our own Whittier, -

> "I know not where His islands lift
> Their fronded palms in air;
> I only know I cannot drift
> Beyond His love and care."

And Baxter agrees with Whittier, —

> "My knowledge of that life is small;
> The eye of faith is dim;
> But 'tis enough that Christ knows all,
> And I shall be with Him."

And, best of all, they both agree with Jesus: "Let not your heart be troubled. . . . In my Father's house are many mansions. . . . I go to prepare a place for you. . . . I will come again, and receive you unto myself; that where I am, there ye may be also."

VII

WHAT IS IT TO BE A CHRISTIAN?

"To be a Christian." — ACTS xxvi. 28.

CHRIST is the pivotal thought, the central fact, in Christianity. The entire system revolves around a person — the Lord Jesus Christ. One has well said, "The person of Jesus Christ comprehends all there is of it, and without this person there is nothing left that is distinctly Christian." Other religions may be entirely separated from the founder or teacher who originated or put them into shape, and yet lose nothing that is essential to them. Not so with Christianity. It is altogether personal. It can in no wise be separated from the person of Jesus Christ. The first great fact lying at the foundation of all discussion of what it is to be a Christian is that Jesus Christ was the first Christian. I have read a homely story some-

WHAT IS IT TO BE A CHRISTIAN? 123

where that illustrates the practical phase of this whole problem.

"The parson asked a strange question this evening," said John Sewell to his wife Ann, on his return from church one Sunday.

"What was it, John?"

"'Who has seen Christ in you to-day?' I wish you had been there to hear him, Ann; he made it pretty plain that all who love Christ ought to show by their conduct that they are in earnest."

"That's true, John. I know I often fall short of what a Christian ought to be."

"I am sure that you and the children have not seen Christ in me to-day. If I'd remembered to be like my Master, I should not have been so cross with you because you wanted to take your turn out this morning."

"And I shouldn't have snapped you up so, and been so vexed," interrupted Ann.

"Then I used Tom roughly because he worried me; and when he cried I boxed his ears, when a kind word would have made all right. There are plenty of things I should have done to-day if I had acted up to the parson's question."

"We'll try to begin fresh, John. You're quick, and I get vexed. We've both a deal to learn. We must just pray that the children and our friends may see Christ in us."

Monday morning came. John was up early; and before he went off to work he asked that Christ might be in him that day. Ann did not forget that she, too, wished that Christ might be seen in her: and at breakfast-time the children were told how Christ might be seen in them, and they were cautioned to be kind towards one another and towards their companions. Thus throughout the family tempers were quelled for Christ's sake, and pleasant acts were performed for Christ's sake; and John was able in that same strength to ask a fellow-workman to forgive the sharp words he had spoken to him the previous Saturday.

"I've had the happiest day I ever spent," John remarked to his wife that evening. "I know I've long been a professor, but I have not shown by my behavior that I do really want Jesus to be seen in me."

"I am sure it has been just the same with me," replied Ann.

"I know why some of our fellows in the shop find fault with religious people, and call them no better than those who have no religion at all. We Christians are not shining lights; we get into the same tempers, and use the same sharp words, and do the same actions, as men of the world, and we bring reproach on Jesus."

"That's well said, John. I mean to ask myself every night, 'Who has seen Christ in me to-day?' I know that I shall often have to tell God that I've failed; but Jesus will help me to be true to Him, and you know there is a text that says, 'I live, yet not I, but Christ liveth in me.'"

Let our foundation stone rest in our minds, then, that first of all a Christian is a man or woman in this world to represent Christ. Let us trace some features of that character drawn in the Gospel which make it proper to call the possessor of it a Christian.

1. A Christian is one who accepts Christ's estimate of character.

Christ makes everything kneel down and worship in the presence of character. Through one of the old prophets God said, "Look not on his countenance, or on the height of his stature: ... for the Lord seeth not as man seeth; for man looketh on the outward appearance, but the Lord looketh on the heart." You remember the Greek story which tells us how the old philosopher, whose soul was filled with disgust at the depravity and folly of his age, in bitter sarcasm went up and down the streets of Athens, at midday, with a lighted lantern in his hand, seeking for an honest man. If he had been a wiser philosopher he would have known that manhood is not discoverable by the light of any earthly lantern. The Gospel represents the standard of divine judgment as depending altogether upon character. If you would find one of the pivotal passages of Bible truth, go to the twelfth chapter of Luke, and read the words of Jesus, "A man's life consisteth not in the abundance of the things which he possesseth." There is a vast difference between the position of the world and the Christian's position at this pivotal point. The world, except so far as Christ has permeated it, exalts everything else above character, setting the things upon and around the manhood above the manhood itself.

The faultlessly dressed young man or young woman of the world passes the plainly clad sage or saint by with a smile of supreme contempt. The unjust judge in many American commonwealths, to-day as in olden times, despises the poor widow who urges her cause before him, but hearkens to the most infamous power in the land, because of "the abundance of the things which that infamous power possesseth." The Dives of to-day, as of yesterday, sees Lazarus at the mercy of the dogs without inquiring into or suspecting the manhood there which holds communion with the angels. Many a scholar holds no intercourse with an ignorant man. A man whose only abundance it may be consists in a white skin, and even that reddened with the wine of wickedness, is full of contempt and disdain for the yellow Chinaman or the red Indian, ready to trample them all alike under his foot, though the one be as wise as Confucius and the other as tender-hearted as Pocahontas. If Jesus of Nazareth Himself, with all His matchless nobility of character, under the guise of a yellow instead of a Jewish face, had been in Seattle last springtime, He would have been pelted through the street with rocks ; or in Wyoming, would have been murdered in His bed, as were some of His faithful followers. But the Christian standard remains, and all the while it is true that the true Christian accepts as his own this Christly standard of judgment — character.

2. Again, the Christian accepts the sacrifice of Christ as the redemption of his personal soul from sin. The fact of sin is sustained by the universal consciousness. The great question everywhere, under all forms of worship, is: "How shall a man be just with God?" That question underlies every heathen temple, every Mohammedan mosque, and every idol shrine on the earth.

A lady was sitting on her veranda in India, reading. She heard the tramp of some one running very fast, and presently a boy bounded into her presence, all out of breath.

"Does Jesus Christ live here?" was his cry.

The lad was about twelve years old. His hair was coarse and matted with filth. His clothes were dirty.

Flying up the steps and crouching at the

lady's feet, he again inquired, "Does Jesus Christ live here?"

"What do you want of Jesus Christ?" she asked.

"I want to see Him. I want to confess to Him," was the reply.

"Why, what have you been doing that you want to confess?"

With great earnestness the boy said, "Does He live here? I want to know that. Doing? Why, I tell lies. I steal. I do everything bad. I am afraid of going to hell, and I want to see Jesus. I heard one of the teachers say He can save from hell. Does He live here? Oh, tell me where I can find Jesus Christ!"

"But Jesus Christ will not save people who do wickedly," said the lady.

"I want to stop doing wickedly, but I cannot stop," said the boy. "I don't know how to stop. The evil thoughts are in me, and the bad deeds come of evil thoughts. What can I do?"

He was told he could do nothing but go to Christ, but that he could not see Christ as he evidently expected to see Him. He was no longer on the earth in bodily form. As he heard this he gave a quick, sharp cry of despair. But he brightened up when the good missionary lady told him she was a follower of Jesus, and that she had come to India on purpose to tell people how to be saved.

"Tell me, oh, tell me about Him!" was his eager cry. "Only ask your Master, the Lord Jesus, to save me, and I will be your servant, your slave, for life. Do not be angry. Do not send me away. I want to be saved, saved from hell."

We may be sure the simple story of the cross was soon told this poor Hindoo lad, and he was easily led to trust with all his heart in Him who came hither to save lost sinners.

The Christian rests his hope of forgiveness and redemption from his sins, entirely, not upon any meritorious conduct of his own, but upon the sacrifice of Jesus, which he regards as a propitiation not for his sins only, but for the sins of the whole world.

Herodotus tells us that when the victorious Cyrus was pushing his conquests towards the east, the various princes of the country resisted him, and that among them was a noble young prince by the name of Tigranes, who gave him more trouble than any of the rest. But at last Tigranes was overcome; and in the evening of the day of the battle Cyrus, seated upon a throne in a large pavilion, received the captives, and looked upon the trophies of his victory as they passed before him. At last came the royal family of Tigranes, consisting of himself and wife and his father and mother. There they stood; and the royal conqueror on the throne looked at them, and asked Tigranes with what he would redeem his father and mother. He offered for them all his remaining treasure, and they were ordered to stand aside. Then there came another question: "Tigranes, with what wilt thou redeem thy wife?" A look of horror, says Herodotus, passed over his manly face as he thought that all was gone, and nothing had been preserved with which to redeem the wife of his love. He knew that according to Oriental custom she was doomed; and so absorbed was he in the misery of the moment, that the question was thrice repeated before he was aroused. At last, lifting his head, he said, "O Cyrus, I will redeem her; I will die for her, if you will restore her to liberty." Such an answer won the respect of Cyrus, and he gave orders for their immediate release. In the evening of that day, as they were conversing together on its eventful scenes, Tigranes turned to his wife and asked her if she was not struck with the noble appearance of Cyrus. A second time was the question asked before she seemed to notice it; and then she answered, "No: I was not looking at Cyrus." "At whom, then," said the surprised Tigranes, "were you looking?" That question filled her heart, and with eyes streaming with tears she answered. "I was looking at the man who offered to redeem me with his life." What to her heart was the splendor of Cyrus and the magnificence of the circumstances in the midst of which she stood? Her husband's love, stronger than death, she saw as vastly more glorious than all the pomp and array of armies or thrones.

And so, my Christian brother, if at last you are so unspeakably happy as to kneel before Him that sitteth on the throne, and cast your crown at His feet, you will say to the angel that kneels by your side, "That is He who redeemed me; not one who in a moment of generosity only was willing to redeem me; but when I was in sin and misery He came down and took upon Himself my nature, and for three and thirty years He tasted my grief and despised the shame and endured the cross and bled upon it for me."

3. The Christian is one who accepts Christ's law of life, which is self-sacrifice for others. And here, again, how wide is the difference between the Christian standard and that of the world!

The world's proverb is, "Every man for himself;" and it only takes the next legitimate step when it adds, "and the devil for us all." It is Christianity which says, "Bear ye one another's burdens, and so fulfil the law of Christ." How blind are those socialistic leaders who seek to lift up the poor and helpless by turning away from Christianity to atheism! Atheism has nothing to offer the poor man but the cruel law of the survival of the fittest. Herbert Spencer, in his "Social Statics," plainly says, "The poverty of the incapable, and the distress which comes upon the imprudent, and the starvation of the idle, and the shouldering aside of the weak by the strong, which leaves so many in the shallows and miseries, is the decree of a large, far-reaching benevolence." How is that for cold-blooded theory? All atheism is a heartless negation of that faith in a loving God and the brotherhood of humanity which is the poor man's strongest plea in the court of civilization.

And yet it may be that the lack of the manifestation of this essential characteristic of Christian character among many of the professed followers of Jesus often helps to turn the discouraged soul towards a heartless speculation. The prevailing sin of the day is self-indulgence. It is a canker that eats the life-blood out of many a Christian life. The treasury of Christ is often robbed in order to devote the gold belonging to it to some idol of fashion or pleasure. It is to most people, perhaps, harder to give up ease than money. Personal exertion to save sinners, or to do the disagreeable duty and to keep at it with cheerful face and heart, is one of the severest tests of Christian self-sacrifice. Blessed is the man or woman who out of an honest, grateful heart can say, "It is my meat and drink to do my Master's will, and to finish the work that He gave me to do."

Dr. Cuyler calls it "the grace that pinches." The daily battle of Christian principle is with that artful, subtle, greedy sinner, *self;* and the highest victory of our religion is to follow Jesus over the rugged path of self-denial. The true disciples of Christianity sing, —

> "Not to ourselves alone,
>   Not to the flesh, we'll live;
> Not to the world shall we
>   Our strength and being give!
>
> No longer be our life
>   A selfish thing, or vain;
> For us, even here, to live be Christ,
>   For us to die is gain."

4. The Christian accepts Christ's love for the soul as its chief inspiration.

There is no inspiration so high as that which the knowledge of love creates. A little child will work wonders under the approving eye of father or mother, whose love is the inspiration of his life. How soldiers have fought on bloody fields to give gladness to the heart of a beloved captain! You have all read of the old Highland chieftain, who fell on the battle-field, pierced by a dozen balls. His clan, thinking he was slain, began to waver. Raising himself upon his elbow as he lay upon the brow of the hill, he called, "My children, I am not dead; I am looking upon you." That cry turned defeat into victory. So the Christian's highest, holiest inspiration springs from the knowledge of Christ's deathless love for him. Nothing can break down his courage while the consciousness of that love buoys his heart.

One of the finest pictures in the Old Testament, which is a great gallery of striking scenes, is the story told of David when he was in the cave of Adullam, which you may find in the twenty-third chapter of Second Samuel. The Philistines were encamped at Rephaim, and at the end of the plain. David had had nothing to drink for twenty-four hours; and as he lay panting in the cave, with his men of arms about him, he said, "Oh, that one would give me drink of the water of the well of Bethlehem, which is by the gate." It was an ejaculation which fierce thirst wrung from him. There were three brave men who at once determined to gratify his wish, and they went over the plain, where the arrows were raining down upon them; but through the midst of the hurtling arrows and flying javelins they went to the well of Bethlehem and got the water, and brought a gourdful of it to the king to slake his thirst. There is nothing grander in the history of man than David's conduct then. He would not drink of it, suffering though he was, but poured it out as a libation to the Lord; and why? My God forbid, said David, that I should drink the blood of these men that have put their lives in jeopardy; for with the jeopardy of their lives they brought it. So the Christian with heart burning with gratitude exclaims in the midst of life's work, "Every hour of this life of mine was purchased at the price of His blood who loved me and gave Himself for me! Shall I drink up in my own selfishness those hours purchased for me? No, indeed; God forbid! But I will pour them out as a libation before the Lord in any work, however severe, to which His voice may call."

5. The Christian accepts loyalty to Christ as the supreme duty, and in its exercise finds his supreme joy. He only is Master.

One of the noblest characteristics of manhood is the loyalty of which it is capable to a great soul. Horace Scudder has recently told an interesting incident in the life of Washington. It was at a time when he was generally very popular. His men worshipped him; the officers nearest to him, and especially those who formed a part of his military family, were warmly attached to him; but in Congress there were men who violently opposed him, and there were certain generals who not only envied him, but were ready to seize any opportunity which might offer to belittle him, and to put one of their own number in his place. The chief men who were engaged in this business were Generals Conway, Mifflin, and Gates; and from the prominent position taken in the affair by the first-named officer, the intrigue against Washington goes by the name of the Conway Cabal. After it had failed of its purpose by various roundabout methods, it looked about in Congress, and counted the disaffected, to get a majority vote

WHAT IS IT TO BE A CHRISTIAN? 139

in favor of a motion to arrest the commander-in-chief. So, at least, the story runs, which from its nature would not be found in any record, but was whispered from one man to another. The day came when the motion was to be tried; the conspiracy leaked out, and Washington's friends bestirred themselves. They needed one more vote. They sent post-haste for one of their number, Governor Morris, who was absent in camp; but they feared they could not get him in time. In their extremity they went to William Duer, a member from New York, who was dangerously ill. Duer sent for his doctor.

"Doctor," he asked, "can I be carried to Congress?"

"Yes; but at the risk of your life," replied the physician.

"Do you mean that I should expire before reaching the place?" earnestly inquired the patient.

"No," came the answer; "but I would not answer for your leaving it alive."

"Very well, sir. You have done your duty, and I will do mine!" exclaimed Duer. "Prepare a litter for me; if you will not, somebody else will, but I prefer your aid."

The demand was in earnest, and Duer had already started when it was announced that Morris had returned, and that he would not be needed. Morris had come direct from the camp, with the latest news of what was going on there. His vote would make it impossible for the enemies of Washington to carry their point; their opportunity was lost, and they never recovered it.

So the Christian is one who is willing to risk life itself in loyalty to his Divine Master. The brightest pictures that illuminate the last two thousand years of human history are those scenes of devotion and loyalty to Jesus which, blessed be God, are not dying, but being re-enacted in every land where Jesus is known.

Wherever a great cause staggers under the opposition of evil, and there is a forlorn hope to be led, there is some hero — a hero like George C. Haddock of Sioux City, Iowa — ready to stand in the breach for Christ's sake, who counts not even his life dear unto himself, but is willing to let his blood run in the gutter in order that poor drunkards for whom Christ died may lie in that gutter no more. In such loyalty the Christian finds supreme joy. There is no joy on earth like that afforded by doing a part of Christ's work in saving men.

The Arctic traveller, George Kennan, paints a most brilliant description of a scene far away in Kamchatka, where a portion of their company had been lost in the snow for several weeks. He and a few others set out on a journey of two hundred miles, in the dead of winter, to find them. It was a terrible journey. The very feet of the dogs left blood-prints on the snow. They pushed on for two hundred miles toward the Anadyr River, by the light of Aurora Borealis, hoping to find them. Finally, he tells us, in the awful stillness of the Arctic midnight, when the thermometer was forty degrees below zero, when they were endeavoring to get a little warmth around the fire of a few roots gathered by the way, he heard a sharp halloo across the waste of snow. He quitted the fire and hastened in the direction of the sound, and he found one of the guides standing by a little iron pipe thrust out of the snow-bank.

He hurried up to it, leaned over it, and shouted down the pipe, then listened. Up from beneath the snow came his own familiar language, "Who's there?" "Then," adds Kennan, "they told us how to find the way into the temporary place in which they were hidden under the snow, and we entered the cavern; and when I saw my companions so nearly perished, and felt that I had saved them, I sank down, overcome with joy, utterly unable to speak or move." So many a man or woman doing some of Christ's work, and finally conscious of rescuing some starving, lost soul, has known what it is to be unutterably full of joy. God grant you, my brethren, that supreme joy in which you seem to take part with the angels in heaven, who rejoice over one sinner that repenteth.

Only one thought more, briefly put, and I am done.

The Christian is one who looks forward to eternal life, whose greatest bliss shall rest in his being like Christ, and with Him forever. Not a great deal is told us about that life. Our language is altogether too poor to paint the blessed picture.

Mrs. Willard, in "Life in Alaska," tells of a little Hydah girl who had a passionate love for the beautiful scenery surrounding her home. She would sit in perfect rapture looking at the mountains, sky, and water. At one point of particular beauty she exclaimed, with her hands on her breast and her eyes aglow, "Oh, my heart gave a great shake!" One of her teachers asked her to sketch the scene at sunset. She sat with an expression of countenance worthy of a great artist. Gazing over the shining deep with softened eyes, she simply said, "I can't draw glory." So even the inspired penman has not been able to draw Glory. We rest in perfect confidence in the blessed promise that though it doth not appear what we shall be, yet when He appears, who is our Lord and our Life, we shall be like Him.

"Earth sings her parables of loss and gain
  In boldest speech;
Yet heights sublime which spirits shall attain
  She cannot reach.
Aerial whispers float o'er land and sea;
'It doth not yet appear what we shall be.'

Her royal purples and her crowns of gold,
  Her white attire,

The sceptred lilies which her summers hold,
   With flames afire —
All fail to show the glory we shall see;
' It doth not yet appear what we shall be.'

Who from unsightly bulb or slender root
   Could guess aright
The glory of the flower, the fern, the fruit,
   In summer's height?
Through tremulous shadows voices call to me,
' It doth not yet appear what we shall be.'

Triumphant guesses from the seer and sage
   Through shadows dart,
And tender meanings on the poet's page
   Console the heart.
Oh, songs prophetic! though so sweet are ye,
' It doth not yet appear what we shall be.' "

VIII

AT THE GATE BEAUTIFUL

"Now Peter and John went up together into the temple at the hour of prayer," etc. — ACTS iii. 1-11.

THIS temple was one of the most magnificent ever built by man. We are told that more than ten thousand skilled workmen were employed upon it. It was built of beautiful white stones, each one of which was forty feet long, fourteen feet high, and twenty feet broad. One of its cloisters was formed of one hundred and sixty-two pillars, fifty feet in height, and each so large as to require three men with arms extended to reach around it. This cloister alone was one hundred feet longer than the Cologne Cathedral. Running around the whole structure, above the gates, was a golden vine with pendent branches, most delicately formed of the same precious metal, so that all who beheld it were filled with amazement. There were nine colossal gates, covered with silver and gold, which gave entrance into that splendid temple; but in magnitude and splendor the one called "the Beautiful" far surpassed all the rest. It was twenty-four feet broad and forty-five feet in height. It was decorated with lilies, formed of Corinthian brass. It opened toward the sunrise, and must have been dazzling indeed with the morning's radiant beams upon it.

Here it was that the crippled man who had been helpless from his infancy was laid to receive the alms of the people as they went in to worship. This whole picture we are to study is dramatic to the last degree. Peter and John themselves are a most interesting pair. There is no more fascinating man in the Bible portrait gallery than Peter. You can pick flaws in him by the hour, but he never bores you. Bold, impetuous, daring, egotistical, but always interesting. Peter reminds me of some great mountain that lifts itself into the clouds, out from the lower range of hills: a mountain formed by some tremendous volcanic upheaval that has left the rude and ragged scars of its creation upon its face. It is too great, too awful, too sublime, to be merely pretty. It is scarred by deep gorges and marred by dark lava ledges; but the everlasting snows crown its dome, about its feet the dark forests grow, and from its heart pour cool, refreshing streams that bless the foothills and the valleys far away. And when the evening sun pours its wealth of color upon the ugly old mountain summit, it is glorified with a grandeur that far surpasses anything that can be called beautiful. So Peter is a man scarred by passion and seamed by sin, but there is something heroic and massive about his great soul; and when at last the full glory of God's transforming love has flooded his life, he glows with a radiance that is divine. Then here is John, the sensitive disciple. Not always a saint by any means — anything but that at the beginning. For he is the man who wished to call down fire from heaven to burn up the town, root and branch, that did not receive his Master. But, like David, John had a teachable soul, easily susceptible to higher influences. One of those refined natures which, in their essential elements, are as delicate as the spirit of a sensitive woman, whose heart is so exactly tuned as to be affected by the slightest breath of influence. John's soul, wrought upon by the Christ, is so dominated by the heavenly Spirit that he comes to be pre-eminently the disciple whom Jesus loves; and, of all places on earth, he was most happy when he could lay his head on Jesus' breast. These are the men who, taken together, represent the genius of Christianity — the daring of faith, and the tenderness of love — who stand before the poor crippled beggar at the Beautiful Gate.

We have here the proper spirit of Christianity. We are to care not only for the people inside the gate, but we are to seek out and care for the crippled lives which are without. If modern Christianity means anything, it means that Jesus Christ is represented in those who call themselves by His name, and who go about doing good, like Peter and John, for His sake, and through the sympathy and power which He gives. Character means service, and the keynote of a Christian life is fruit. The true aim of a Christian life is not peace, though it shall have peace; it is not joy, though Christ declared His joy should not be taken away from us; it is not rest, or happiness, though His promise to the heavy-laden and careworn is that by coming to Him they shall find rest unto their souls; but the great end of the Christian life is fruit-bearing. Usefulness is commensurate with the Christian life. A fruitless Christian is a useless Christian. Christ compares His relation to us with the relation of a vine to its branches. The vine is the strong and upholding centre, gathering up nourishment, and sending its life pulsating through all the branches: but all the clusters of grapes hang on the branches. It is just as true to say that the vine can do nothing without the branches as it is to say that the branches can do nothing without the vine. Our Lord Jesus Christ intends to bring about the reign of righteousness in this world through His disciples. Cornelius and his family were brought into happy Christian experience by the power and grace of Christ; but not until Peter had preached to them the word. The treasurer of Queen Candace was baptized with great joy into the faith of the Gospel; but not until Philip, sitting by his side in the chariot, had pointed him from prophecy to fulfilment in the cross and the sundered tomb. Saul was changed to Paul largely by that wonderful vision on the way to Damascus; but his eyes were not opened until faithful Ananias bent over him in prayerful benediction. Christ reaches men through men; and He is looking after the sorrowing, the sick, the afflicted, and oppressed now, as in the days when He was on earth, and in the later days of the apostles, through men and women who, having caught His spirit and owned Him Lord, go forth to take His place in the dusty highways of common life. William Carey, going to India, is there the representative of Jesus. Dorothy Dix, going from land to land and from dungeon to dungeon, looking after Christ's neglected poor among the insane, changing the attitude of the whole race toward this afflicted class, was simply representing Jesus Christ. John Howard, going down into the prisons of the Old World, and hunting out the forgotten and neglected multitudes hidden away from the world's view, and calling the attention of mankind to horrors and cruelties of which the great mass of the people had never dreamed, was only exemplifying the declaration of Jesus that His disciples were to be the light of the world. Florence Nightingale, in the Crimea, whether cutting the axe through the red tape that locked storehouse doors against sick and starving soldiers, or bowing and smiling down the long lines of wounded and dying in the hospital, where many a homesick soldier would turn and kiss her shadow where it fell on his pillow, was simply living out in real life the sisterhood of Jesus Christ. Coming closer into our own day, Loring Brace, with his Children's Aid Society, and the multitudes of tender and sympathetic souls who have followed in his footsteps ; and Henry Bergh, with his self-denying life given over to the protection of dumb beasts from cruel hands ; and the hospitals and almshouses and orphan asylums and houses of refuge and day nurseries, which are coming ever more rapidly to be points of heavenly light in the midst of our large cities and towns, bear their own sweet testimony that the pitiful, tender Christ has not left the world, but still walks among men ever to do good.

There is something most fascinating to me in the daring faith of these disciples as they turn to give their great help to this poor cripple. You see in this very spirit the power which made it possible for Christianity to overrun the then known world, and conquer the Roman Empire, in spite of all opposition, within the first two or three centuries. Brothers and sisters, that is the spirit which above everything else we need!

A distinguished professor in one of our colleges, writing in a popular review not long ago, takes up the sad refrain which is altogether too common in our time — "it is a tough old world;" and the substance of his conclusion is, that because the world is so "tough," we had better leave it alone and spare our foolish pains. Thank God, that is not the Christian way of regarding great tasks. Somebody has said that all men are to be divided into two classes — those to whom nothing is possible, and those to whom all things are possible. The Christian belongs to the latter class; for his Bible tells him that "all things are possible to him that believeth." A leading man in Chicago said, the other day, "I have lived in Chicago now thirty odd years, and in that time it has been the crazy men who have become rich; the men who thought it was impossible that this swamp should be converted into a metropolis are poor to-day." It is so in our work for God. The men who bring things to pass in pulling down the strongholds of sin and in winning souls to Christ, are the men who believe that the mightiest forces in the world are the forces that work for righteousness. Ignorant men talk about the power of a cyclone, but the scientist knows that the power which builds up a forest is a thousand times mightier than that which uproots a tree; that that which tosses a house in the air is but a feeble thing compared with the splendid force which swings a million stars through the depths of space and never loses track of one of them for a moment. So men who see only sensual and earthly things, and know nothing of the great spiritual Heart of the universe, tell us that it is impossible that we should ever overthrow the liquor traffic, or stamp out the lottery or the gambling hells, and make proverbs like this: "Every man has his price;" which is only a coarse way of saying that the mean and vulgar passions are the most powerful forces that touch man's nature. But the Christian knows that this is not true. He knows that faith and hope and love are more than a match for greed and selfishness and lust. And he stands before the poor, crippled souls, marred and scarred and dwarfed by sin's vicious and ugly hand, and, like Peter, does not fear to attempt their transformation in the name of Jesus Christ. For of all the passions of the human soul, love — not selfishness nor hate — is supreme. Scarcely a day passes in which the newspapers do not record some heroic death for the sake of love. Now it is a father snatching his boy from the flames; again, a mother dying upon a track where her babe had wandered; but always and everywhere love is the strongest and the sweetest thing in the world. The people who are making their poor sneer of contempt at the daring claim that the Cross of Jesus Christ can conquer this "tough old world," do not know the splendid force which animates millions of men and women who are ready to live and die in loving devotion

to the Christ who died to redeem them. May
God baptize this church with this daring spirit,
and make us in these streets of Brooklyn like
Peter and John were at the gate of the old
temple — the channels through which Christ's
healing power may come!

The most splendid thing about this scene at
the Beautiful Gate was not the beauty of the
temple or of the gate itself, nor even the faith
and courage of Peter and John, but the glorious
manifestation of the power of Jesus Christ in
the cure of the sick man, who, healed in body
and soul, went leaping into the temple, praising
God. It may be that I am preaching to some
who are conscious as I speak that this crippled
man at the temple gate is a type of their spiritual condition: it may be that in your inmost
soul you are conscious that at the beautiful gate
of the Gospel your nature, crippled by sin and
wicked habits, lies impotent and helpless. Ah,
if such is the case, I thank God that you are
conscious of it; and if there be any here who
are sick with sin, but who, hiding under pride
and indifference, are stifling conscience and
refusing to hear its reproofs, I pray God that

the Holy Spirit may make you conscious of your great need. There is nothing more pitiable than to see a man who is spiritually bankrupt, and whose better nature is swamped in sin, who yet fondly imagines that he does not need the forgiving mercy of Jesus Christ. Many there are, like the church of the Laodiceans described in Revelation, of whom God looking down on them says, "Because thou sayest, I am rich, and increased with goods, and have need of nothing; and knowest not that thou art wretched, and miserable, and poor, and blind, and naked: I counsel thee to buy of me gold tried in the fire, that thou mayest be rich; and white raiment, that thou mayest be clothed, and that the shame of thy nakedness do not appear; and anoint thine eyes with eyesalve, that thou mayest see. As many as I love, I rebuke and chasten: be zealous therefore, and repent. Behold, I stand at the door and knock: if any man hear my voice, and open the door, I will come in to him, and will sup with him, and he with me. . . . He that hath an ear, let him hear." How the cured cripple must have looked back many a time to that one great hour of opportunity which brought him healing and salvation. If you will open your hearts to hear the word, this may be your hour of transformation and blessing. The Rev. Robert McIntyre, of Denver, one of the most brilliant men in the pulpit to-day, recently told the story of his conversion. He was born in Scotland, and his parents brought him to this country when he was small. His father died early, and he learned the trade of a bricklayer, and became the bread-earner for his mother and brothers. He drifted into infidelity, and became a leader of infidel clubs. In St. Louis, where his home was, a friend prevailed on him one Monday evening to attend a church service. The minister had scarcely begun to preach when, Dr. McIntyre says, "For the first time in my life I heard a man preaching to me, and in ten minutes I was trembling from head to foot. I know the Holy Spirit had hold of me. I was introduced to the preacher, and I said I would like to have a talk with him, for his sermon had greatly moved me. He told me where he lived, and asked me to call the next day. I went, and we talked together for two hours. I advanced my infidel arguments, and he sought to reply; but I thought I had got the better of him, and when I rose to go I told him I was worse than when I came. He said, 'Do you mean to tell me I have failed to do you good?' and I said, 'That is exactly what you have done, sir.' He said, 'Do you know, sir, that I expected to fail?' Then he said, 'But I have a friend who never fails in these matters.' I did not understand Gospel phraseology, and so I innocently asked, 'Where is he?' He said, 'Right here,' and then he said, 'Let us kneel down right here and pray;' and before I really knew what I was doing, I was on my knees. In a moment I saw I had lost the battle. When he talked to me I could answer him, but when he prayed I could not say a word; and, oh, how he prayed! It reminded me of my brother's prayer for me years before. But I would not yield. On leaving him I said, 'I wish you would preach at the church to-morrow night.' He said, 'I will if you will be there,' and I promised to go.

"Every word he said in that second sermon seemed like a barbed arrow in my heart. After the sermon the usual invitation was given for seekers while a hymn was sung. I clutched the bench in front of me to keep from shaking. I could scarcely breathe. I said to myself, If I ever get into the street again, I will forever keep away from this church. My friend Grant was behind me, and touching me on the shoulder he said, 'Go to the altar.' But the devil was rampant in me, and my teeth were set, and I would not move. The preacher said, 'Sing another verse; there may be some here in the valley of decision.' Though trembling like an aspen leaf, I refused to move. He then lifted up his hands and said, 'We have done all we can,' and began to pronounce the benediction.

"Something within me said, 'If that benediction is pronounced, and you go out unsaved, it is the day of judgment for you.' While the benediction was on his lips I jumped out into the aisle and ran as if the devil was after me, and fell at the altar, for I had not strength enough to kneel. For a few minutes I did not know anything. When I came to myself they were singing, 'Jesus loves you just now;' and it seemed to me it was the sweetest singing I ever heard. It seemed that a great avalanche of rock had slipped down on me, and I felt bound to the floor. I could hardly breathe, but was trying to pray. It seemed that I would die if I could not get relief. An old gray-haired mother in Israel came and knelt beside me and heard me cry, 'O God, help me!' and she said, 'Do not pray that way; God will not hear that prayer. Say this: O God, for Jesus' sake have mercy on me.' I took the very words from her lips, and repeated them; and then the great mountain lifted from me, and my heart burst into raptures of joy. Tears streamed down my face, and all my darkness went away. Such a sense of victory filled the room that all knew that the work was done."

Are there not some who will catch inspiration from the story of this glorious conversion, and yield your own hearts to Christ here and now? Are you not ready to pray with Lucy Larcom, —

> "Lord, open the door, for I falter,
> I faint in this stifled air;
> In dust and straitness I lose my breath;
> This life of self is a living death.

AT THE GATE BEAUTIFUL

Let me into Thy pastures broad and fair,
To the sun and the wind from Thy mountains free;
Lord, open the door to me!

There is holier life, and truer,
Than ever my heart has found;
There is nobler work than is wrought within
These walls so charred by the fires of sin,
Where I toil like a captive blind and bound —
An open door to a freer task
In Thy nearer smile, I ask.

. . . .

Yet crippled and dumb, behold me wait,
Dear Lord, at the Beautiful Gate!

I wait for Thy hand of healing —
For vigor and hope in Thee.
Open wide the door — let me feel the sun —
Let me touch Thy robe — I shall rise and run
Through Thy happy universe, safe and free,
Where in and out Thy beloved go,
Nor want nor wandering know.

Thyself art the Door most holy!
By Thee let me enter in!
I press toward Thee with my failing strength
Unfold Thy love in its breadth and length!
True life from Thine let my spirit win.

. . . .

Life! Life! I may enter, through Thee, the Door,
Saved, sheltered forevermore!"

IX

THE NOBILITY OF SERVICE

" For David, after he had served his own generation by the will of God, fell on sleep, and was laid unto his fathers." — Acts xiii. 36.

WHAT is it to live?

" To feed on flesh and eat the oaten cake,
   Made by the cunning of the housewife's hands,
Stopping from toil to soothe the pains which ache
   With cooling lotions and repressive bands,
And scarce a moment rid of care to find
Proper refreshment for the starving mind —
          Is this to live?

Or is't to feast with Epicurean skill
   On potted meats, drinking huge draughts of wine;
Giving to greed the loosest rein, until,
   Filled with disease and racked by pain, supine
The body lies, waiting untimely death,
The passing out of the last passing breath —
          Is this to live?

Or is't to robe in butterfly array
   This mortal dust, and make a spectacle
Of pride for envy; frittering away
   Valuable time in what must ever dull

> The soul's keen vision of the good and pure,
> Which lasts fore'er, as grace and truth endure —
>   Is this to live?
>
> Or is't to drink at faith's unfailing stream;
>   Obey the Lord's and duty's high command;
> Converse in heaven, and on its glories dream;
>   And upward lift forever prayerful hands,
> Waiting with service for the exit here,
> The death-like entrance upon glory there?
>   'Tis this to live."

Our human life has to do with two worlds. Dr. Kelley tells the story of a little black beetle that swims on the summer brook, well known to all of us who have lived in the country. This creature loves to hold insect conventions in quiet nooks or eddies, and for hours glide and whirl about in all manner of fantastic gyrations. One curious thing about this insect is, that it has two pairs of eyes; and, as it floats along, one pair of eyes is below the water, and the other is above it. The one pair to review things below, and the other above, the surface. The one looks out for food, and the other, not only for enemies, but enjoyment as well. These two pairs of eyes together fit the insect for its life on the dividing line between the air and the water. So God has designed us to live in this world, on the border line between the material and the spiritual. We cannot be altogether in either, just now, without damage to some part of our nature. We, too, are endowed with two sets of eyes — bodily and spiritual. We are not only to use the eyes that search out food for the body, but above all we are to develop strength and keenness of perception in those eyes that look into the realm from whence come not only our chief enemies, but also our truest enjoyment and noblest friends.

We have as our text this morning an epitaph in memory of David, written by the Apostle Paul. That which first impresses itself upon us is that Paul gives as the chief characteristic of David's life the fact of service.

I.

And it is true that the supreme purpose of life is to serve. Jesus made that teaching certain. "The Son of man came not to be ministered unto, but to minister." Whenever a life is planned upon any other basis than to make it a helper in the world's work, it is planned not only to be useless, but to be dangerous. It is a sad thing to see so many men and women of intelligence and capability who deliberately plan to live lives of simply selfish gratification. Such people are only dead branches on the fruitful tree of civilization.

In making our human lives hinge on service, God is true to the nature of things. Only by service can we find the true joy and enthusiasm of living. The story is told of a young German nobleman, heir to large estates, who after his college course travelled far and wide: saw, heard, and enjoyed everything, and then returned to his native place. One day, some time after his return, he declared to his friend, a manufacturer, that he was tired of life, and was going to commit suicide that very night. His friend, who was a man of sense and discretion, requested him, as a last favor, to come and see his factory before committing the fatal act. It was the busy season, and the workmen were working till twelve at night. The young nobleman came, and his friend had ordered things so that, immediately on his entrance, certain workmen seized him, clapped a blouse on him, and compelled him to work like the others.

The nobleman, on finding remonstrance vain, did as he was bid; and, after toiling until he was covered with perspiration, the lunch was ordered. This consisted of black bread, sausage, and root beer. The nobleman ate this plain food with an appetite such as the finest viands had never caused him to feel. One workman came up to him and said, "Friend, you see before you the father of five children. I lost three of them at one sweep. I was almost crazy, and wished to die. But I had to work for the other two, who are dearer to me than life itself. Now working for them has helped me to forget my lost, and made life sweet to me again. I have overcome my grief for the others." The nobleman listened, saw, and felt. He remembered that he had large estates and many tenants, and could do an immense amount of good; so he determined to devote his energies to improving his estates and the condition of the tenantry upon them; and, as the fairy stories say, lived happy ever afterward. But there is a lesson in the story — a deep and true one, which he who runs may read.

It is the duty of every one of us to do the

best work of which we are capable, and to exert the best possible influence on humanity. And we serve ourselves best in thus serving others. A true life lives in the happiness it creates, and derives its joy from the service of God and others. Such lives were never in greater demand than now. Every great cause is echoing and re-echoing the poet's call, —

> "Wanted: men.
> Not systems fit and wise,
> Not faiths with rigid eyes,
> Not wealth in mountain piles,
> Not power with gracious smiles,
> Not even the potent pen;
>   Wanted: men.
>
> Wanted: Deeds.
> Not words of winning-note,
> Not thoughts of life remote,
> Not fond religious airs,
> Not sweetly languid prayers,
> Not love of scented creed;
>   Wanted: deeds.
>
> Men and deeds —
> Men that can dare and do,
> Not longings for the new,
> Not prating for the old;
> Good life and action bold,
> These the occasion needs;
>   Men and deeds."

The path of service is open to all, nay, we stumble on to the path daily without knowing it.

Ivan Tourguenieff, in one of his beautiful poems in prose, says, "I was walking in the street; a beggar stopped me — a frail old man. His inflamed, tearful eyes, blue lips, rough rags, disgusting sores — oh, how horribly poverty had disfigured the unhappy creature! He stretched out to me his red, swollen, filthy hands; he groaned and whimpered for alms. I felt in all my pockets; no purse, watch, or handkerchief did I find; I had left them all at home. The beggar waited, and his outstretched hand twitched and trembled. Embarrassed and confused, I seized his dirty hand and pressed it. 'Don't be vexed with me, brother: I have nothing with me, brother.' The beggar raised his bloodshot eyes to mine; his blue lips smiled, and he returned the pressure of my chilled fingers. 'Never mind, brother,' stammered he; 'thank you for this — this, too, was a gift, brother.' I felt that I, too, had received a gift from my brother."

This is a line of service open to us all.

However poor we may be in earthly possessions, we may at least be rich in that fulness of humanity which recognizes the manhood and womanhood of every one with whom we come in contact. And there is no reason for discouragement because the service we offer seems small and unimportant. Does not the Master declare that not even a cup of cold water given in the name of a true disciple shall pass unnoticed? And there are thousands of people in our towns and cities who need just that cup of cold water, given in hearty fellowship, to arouse again their hope and courage. The poet tells us of a poor discouraged man who, —

"Stood in fierce despair — gaunt, hollow-eyed,
    With murder whispering in his tortured ear.
No work! his baby's cry broke down his pride,
    His sick wife's pleading brought the horror near.

They heard his tale, and carelessly they threw
    A golden coin, as if they thought the sting
That drove his soul crime's hated portal through,
    Would weaken at the money's golden ring.

His thin face settled in a hateful frown;
    The sneering charity unheeded lay;
They who had idly crushed his manhood down
    Will wonder at his dark revenge some day.

A man with coat as ragged as his own
  Held out a hand and spoke brave words of cheer,
And, lo! the dark, stern face has gentler grown,
  And in the hollow eye there shines a tear.

Forgotten are the hideous thoughts that filled
  His soul; the way seems brighter than before;
A newer courage all his life has thrilled,
  And thrown a gleam of sunshine through hope's door.

He gives the most who bravely lends a hand
  To help his brother in the hour of need;
God keeps the record, — He can understand,
  And of our slightest service will take heed."

II.

We have suggested here, also, the proper sphere of our human lives. Paul says of David that he "served his own generation." The triumphant helpfulness of David's life lay in his promptness to do each duty faithfully, whether it were small or great. He was just as enthusiastic and brave as a keeper of sheep as he was as a warrior doing battle with giants. He seized the present duty promptly. He went out to the army of Israel when they were cowed and afraid, and trying in vain to devise some means by which to slay Goliath. The thought struck David in a moment that there was only one way to kill that big fellow with his heavy armor, and that was to strike him in the one spot where he was unprotected. He saw the great, broad forehead uncovered. He said to himself, " There is my chance to save this army." He was an expert with a sling. He had practised with it till he could sling a stone straight to the mark. He did not stop to hold any council of war about it. He seized promptly hold of his thought, and went to his victory.

There is a later historical incident illustrating youthful promptness and fidelity to the duty at hand that I always associate in my mind with David's defence of Israel against Goliath. It is an incident which occurred in the outbreak of the Sepoy mutiny in 1857. Just before the awful storm broke, the system of electric telegraphs had been extended over the surface of British India. The mutineers rushed to Delhi to seize upon the old hereditary seat of the Mohammedan Empire, and began cutting the throats of Europeans. While the rattle of cannon and musketry was rolling around the telegraph office, a little English boy, moved by the English sense of duty, stuck to his post until he had telegraphed to the commissioner at Lahore. The message announced that the mutineers had arrived at Delhi, and had murdered this civilian and that officer, and wound up with these significant but childish words, " We're off ! " The boy's courage and sense of duty saved the Punjab. That little boy at Delhi saved Northern India to the British crown.

That is always the key to success — do the duty that calls at once.

Carlyle never uttered a keener truth than when he said, " Take an occasion by the foretop; she has no back hair." The cause of righteousness in the world needs just now a re-enforcement of such prompt and earnest souls. Brother, lend it thine ! As one has well said, God needs for to-day " men like Elijah, carrying into the very midst of the Baal worship of modern society the true God in their own devout lives ; men like James the Just, thrusting their defiant Christian honesty in the very face of our day's falsehood and fraud : like Daniel and his friends, shining with speckless purity amid the beastly indulgence and unchastity of the modern cities;

men daring to say 'no' to their own party when wrong; men honorably generous to say 'yes' to opponents when right; men bold enough to take the robbed Indian or the maltreated Chinaman by the hand, and in the very humanity of living Christianity to say, 'I am a man and a brother;' men ready to battle, and, if need be, die, for their country's unity and honor; and yet men with the courage of their convictions, calm and resolute to face the howling mob or the highest bar of their land, and say, 'We ought to obey God rather than men;' men of sober mind and keen eye; men of the clinched fist and firm-set jaw and the iron will; men who stand squarely on the broad, breezy foundations of strong common sense let deeply down into the living rock of eternal truth, and so standing, will say, 'None of these things of public clamor, or party selfishness, or mean suspicions, move us.'"

Such men will be ready to face the living questions that confront us in this hour. They will not shrink in the presence of the liquor question, the tenement-house evil, the infernal sweat-shop, or the wicked threatenings of the gold god. They will dare to believe that Jesus Christ has a mission to municipal and state politics; and will prove themselves the country's fresh heroes.

God grant us more men and women who are not afraid to stand alone, or with the few! The prophet-hearted and resolute young men and women who lead minorities to-day will triumphantly lead the majorities of to-morrow. I would that I had the power to arouse some young David here and now! Some young man yet with the dew of his youth upon him, and the holy fires of his fresh enthusiasm all unspent, and who will dare to face with all joy the Goliaths of our own time.

III.

We have also in this brief epitaph the supreme rule of life. David not only served his own generation, but he served according to "the will of God."

Many of you recall the sweet old legend of St. Christopher, which is so beautifully perpetuated in art in the cathedral at Cologne. A giant had heard of Christ, and was seeking to work out his own salvation by good works. He lived in a cave near a rapid stream; and whoever desired to cross it he took upon his shoulders and bore to the opposite shore. Many a burden he bore wearily across the river, struggling manfully with the waves. But fiercer than the rushing waters were the billows that swept over his own soul, tossing forever with the unrest of a burdened spirit. This penance gave no relief; the river washed no guilt from his heart. The greater the danger in crossing the river, the more willing was he to brave the perilous waves. Whenever he heard a call, he straightway went to aid the traveller, so eager was he to do the work of penance. But good and true and generous as was his work, it did not bring him peace.

One night, being weary, he had fallen asleep in his lonely cave. Without, it was dark and stormy and cold. The river raged fiercely; not a star lighted the night. Above the roar of waters and the howling of the winds he heard a cry of distress. It came from the other side of the river; and it was a child's voice. He had never heard that voice before, nor one like it. It called piteously, "Take me across the river!"

For the first time since he had taken up this life of toil he felt reluctant to go out into the storm and darkness and ford the rushing stream. But before his heart hardened the voice came again — a pleading voice, soft and flute-like, yet entering into the depths of his very soul. Then to his spirit came the words: "Take my yoke upon you, and learn of me, and ye shall find rest unto your soul."

These words were strange to this giant hermit. But a new power tugged at his heart; and, leaving his bed on the cold ground, he took his long pole and went out into the darkness to obey the call. It was only a child; he felt sure of that; it would be nothing to the burdens he so often bore across the river. So, despite his weariness, he went out into the storm. As he looked into the wild night, and plunged into the dangerous river, he still heard the voice. When he had gained the other bank, he found there a child of wonderful beauty, holding his hands out to him and still calling to him: "Come, take me on your shoulders." About the head of this child was a halo, like a crown made of stars. The giant stood for a moment filled with wonder; then, kneeling at his feet, he found himself still too high for the child to climb upon his shoulders. So he threw himself prone upon the earth before him, begging him to put his arms about his neck, and cling fast, while he should bear him safely through the foaming waters to the other shore.

The storm had grown more fierce, the night more dark, and the danger more frightful. Now and then the giant lost his foothold, and at times his staff would not cling to the rocky bed of the river. But the child would whisper, "Fear not; I am with thee," and he took courage again. Then into his soul came the words, "My righteousness." What did it mean? The giant had been trying to establish his own righteousness. Just as he was plunging into a deeper flood, and the current was too strong for him, the child's sweet voice said, "When thou passest through the waters I will be with thee." Then he knew that it was the Lord Christ, the child Jesus, whom he had upon his shoulders.

Now he went on triumphantly. Into the cave

he went, with the child still on his back. And the Christ-child gave him the name "Christopher" — "Christ-bearer." Since then he has had peace in his soul, and has ever been known as St. Christopher.

Shall we not learn St. Christopher's lesson, and pray God that the barrier of our own selfish will that keeps out His precious guiding presence may be broken? Susan Coolidge sweetly sings our truth, —

> "Thy kingdom here?
> Lord, can it be?
> Searching and seeking everywhere
> For many a year,
> 'Thy kingdom come' has been my prayer —
> Was that dear kingdom all the while so near?
>
> Blinded and dull
> With selfish sin,
> Have I been sitting at the gates
> Called Beautiful,
> Where Thy fair angel stands and waits,
> With hand upon the lock, to let me in?
>
> Was I the wall
> Which barred the way,
> Darkening the glory of Thy grace,
> Hiding the ray
> Which, shining out as from Thy very face,
> Had shown to other men the perfect day?

> Was I the bar
> Which shut me out
> From the full joyance which they taste,
> Whose spirits are
> Within Thy paradise embraced —
> Thy blessed paradise, which seems so far?
>
> Let me not sit
> Another hour,
> Idly awaiting what is mine to win,
> Blinded in wit.
> Lord Jesus, rend these walls of self and sin,
> Beat down the gate, that I may enter in."

IV.

Finally, we have life's close as it comes to the one who trusts in God — "He fell on sleep."

"Oh, if I were lucky enough to call this estate mine, I should be a happy fellow!" said a young man.

"And then?" said a friend.

"Why, then I'd pull down the old house and build a palace, have lots of prime fellows around me, keep the best wines and the finest horses and dogs in the country."

"And then?"

"Then I'd hunt and ride and smoke and dance and keep open house and enjoy life gloriously."

" And then ? "

" Why, then, like other people, I should grow old, and not care so much for these things."

" And then ? "

" Why, then, I suppose, in the course of nature, I should leave all these pleasant things — and — well, yes — die ! "

" And then ? "

" Oh, bother your ' thens ' ! I must be off."

Many years after the friend was accosted with, " God bless you ! I owe my happiness to you !"

" How ? "

" By two words spoken in season, long ago, — ' and then ? ' "

Where and how we are to sleep at night may not specially interest us in the morning of vigor, or amid the anxiety of noontide care: but as the sun, with ever westering wheel, turns downward toward the night, it becomes a matter of solemn moment.

> "There comes a time to every mortal being,
> Whate'er his station or his lot in life,
> When his sad soul yearns for the final freeing,
> From all this jarring and unlovely strife.

> There comes a time when, having lost its savor,
>   The salt of wealth is worthless. When the mind
> Grows wearied with the world's capricious favor,
>   And sighs for something that it does not find."

In such a time God "giveth his beloved sleep." As a ripe apple falls lightly with sweet autumn fragrance into the gardener's hand, so do those who have served their generation according to the will of God fall into the hand of the Divine Gatherer.

In the conflict at Waterloo an English soldier, mortally wounded, was carried to the rear by his comrades, and at some distance from the battle-field was laid down under a tree. The dying man asked to have his knapsack opened, that he might obtain his pocket Bible. He then requested a comrade to read to him, before he should breathe his last, from the words of Jesus: "Peace I leave with you, my peace I give unto you; not as the world giveth, give I unto you. Let not your heart be troubled, neither let it be afraid." "Now," said the dying soldier, "I die happy. I desired to have peace with God, and I possess the peace which passeth all understanding."

As the hair whitens about the Christian's brow, he thinks more of death and of the time when he is going home. It seems very natural that Longfellow, in an old age made sweet by his simple trust in God, should have written, —

> "Life to me is a station wherein a traveller stands —
>   One absent long from home and nation
>   In foreign lands;
>   Like him who stands apart and listens
>   Amid the twilight's deep'ning gloom,
>   And hears approaching in the distance
>   The train for home."

X

LUCY STONE

A HEROINE OF THE STRUGGLE FOR HUMAN RIGHTS — THE WOMAN AND HER WORK

"She is like the merchants' ship." — Prov. xxxi. 14.

OUR text is the figure used to describe a good woman by a man who lived many years ago, but who knew much of humanity and was wise in the knowledge of life.

We have just watched a beautiful ship pass safely into port, after a long and sometimes tempestuous voyage. The sails, despite all the experiences of wind and weather, were as white as when given to the breeze more than threescore and ten years ago. The cargo was rich and abundant. No port has been touched in all this voyage but has yielded something to the precious freightage of this queenly ship. At every port, and to every ship hailed on the high seas, something has been given of rich supply; but giving has enriched and not impoverished. The voyage throughout has been against the current and tide; but the ship has been stanch, the helm true, and a braver captain never held a wheel.

In fact, it seems to me that in talking about Lucy Stone I must begin there, because it impresses me most. She was a fearless soul. Her consecration to her work, to her sense of duty, was so complete that it mastered her, and she was its most obedient servant. There was about her none of the bluster and self-assertion that sometimes attend upon courage, but oftener cover up secret cowardice. She was simplicity itself, but as brave a warrior in heart as ever led forlorn hope into the mouth of death-dealing battery. Mrs. Mary A. Livermore recalls how Gilbert Haven, himself a sort of connoisseur on the subject of moral courage, once said to her that he believed Lucy Stone was the one woman in the world who would go to the stake and die for woman suffrage. "'Would you, Mrs. Livermore?' he asked me. And I said I was sure I would not — for it is coming, coming, all in good time. 'But that,' said Gilbert Haven, 'isn't Lucy's way of giving herself wholly to a cause. She would go to the stake and die to get suffrage for women next week.'"

In her heroic living Lucy Stone did many things that were greater tests than dying for her fidelity to the sacred cause of equal rights. All her young life was one constant martyrdom to principle. In these days it is hard to put ourselves back into her place, and understand what it meant to her delicately strung, sensitive soul to be called a fool and crazy, because she longed for an education. There is no more courageous and truly heroic life in American history than this. See that young girl with all the centuries against her, prejudice, conservatism, ignorance, and poverty all frowning upon her, yet gathering her seemingly helpless resources together to fight against all odds. To me it is as splendid as David before Goliath. Watch her as she gathers chestnuts and picks berries, hoarding each precious penny, that it may help to buy books and assist her on toward college. See her on the way — not in the steamer cabin, but sleeping on the grain-sacks among the horses and freight. Go with her as she earns her board doing housework at three cents an hour; living during her college course on fifty cents a week; having only one new dress during the entire course (and that a cheap print), and not seeing her friends at home throughout the entire four years. At last she is graduated at the head of her class, and is offered the commencement oration, provided she will let a man read it; and then the splendid courage of the woman shines out, for she refuses the honor unless she can deliver her own paper, just as a generation later she refused to vote on the school question unless she could vote in her own name.

She became an accomplished Greek and Hebrew scholar, that she might know whether it were true or not that the Bible sanctions the cruel injustice of the feudal ages toward women, and ever after maintained that it was on the side of equal rights for men and women.

Her early life as an agitator was also hard, almost beyond our power to comprehend in these days, when so many women are the honored representatives of the noblest institutions of our time, and plead all good causes with an eloquence and a logic which no one thinks of calling in question. But it was very different before Lucy Stone and her coadjutors pioneered a path and blazed a way through the forest of prejudice. She arranged her own meetings; put out her own handbills with a little package of tacks that she carried, driving the tacks in with a stone picked up in the streets; and she took up her own collections. When she passed the night in Boston she used to stay at a boarding-house on Hanover Street, where she was lodged for six cents, sleeping three in a bed with the young daughters of the house.

A Malden minister being asked to give notice of one of her meetings, did so in the following words: "I am asked to give notice that a hen will attempt to crow like a cock in the town hall at five o'clock to-morrow night. Those who like such music will, of course, attend."

At a meeting in Connecticut, one cold night, a pane of glass was removed from the church window, and through a hose she was suddenly deluged from head to foot with cold water in the midst of her speech; but she wrapped a shawl about her and went on with her lecture.

At an open-air meeting on Cape Cod, where there were a number of speakers, the mob gathered with such threatening violence that all the speakers slipped away, one by one, until no one was left but Stephen Foster.

"You had better go, Stephen," said Lucy, "they are coming."

At that moment the mob made a rush, and one of the ringleaders, a big man with a club, sprang upon the platform.

Lucy turned to him and said in a sweet voice, without any sign of fear, "This gentleman will take care of me."

The man declared that he would. Tucking her under one arm and holding his club in the other hand, he marched her through the crowd, which was roughly using Mr. Foster and the other speakers who had been caught. More than this, Lucy so won upon her protector that the big fellow mounted her on a stump and stood by with his club while she addressed the mob upon the enormity of their conduct. So effective was this address that they took a collection of twenty dollars to pay for Mr. Foster's coat, which they had torn to pieces.

A great debt of gratitude is due to Lucy Stone for her heroic struggle for free speech. A world's temperance convention was held in New York city as late as 1853, which spent nearly the entire time in an acrimonious debate which ended in excluding a delegate because she was a woman. In summing up the proceedings of these meetings Horace Greeley says, in the *Tribune* of Sept. 7, 1853: —

"This convention has completed three of its four business sessions, and the results may be summed up as follows: —

"*First day* — Crowded a woman off the platform.

"*Second day* — Gagging her.

"*Third day* — Voting that she shall stay gagged."

But the woman would not stay gagged, and to-day the largest and most splendidly organized temperance army in the world is the Woman's Christian Temperance Union, led by those twin generals of reform, Frances Willard and Isabel Somerset, which is tying its bows of ribbon white around the world; but let it never be forgotten that the quiet but persistent steps of Lucy Stone marked the way for the coming of these triumphant hosts.

Yet along with this dauntless courage there went a modesty that was as genuine as it was charming. I remember being in the *Woman's Journal* office a few years ago, when Lucy Stone was talking with her old friend, Julia Ward Howe, and myself about a meeting where we were to speak together — in Newport, I think. When asked if she would not also speak, she cheerily replied, "Only for a few minutes. They will want to hear the new voices, and I am only a plain brown wren any way." Mrs. Howe, with delightful sweetness of manner and quick wit, replied, "If I remember correctly, the little brown wren has a most exquisite song of her own."

Lucy Stone's great work was to put the emphasis on the right of every individual, without regard to sex, to have the mastery of his or her destiny. In making this emphasis she was oftentimes misunderstood. It was to put the emphasis distinctly on this important point that on the occasion of her marriage to Mr. Blackwell she declined to assume his name, in which decision he thoroughly acquiesced.

On their marriage they issued to the world a protest which clearly set forth their standpoint, and was in every way honorable to them both. I think it will not be uninteresting to us to recall it here : —

> While acknowledging our mutual affection by publicly assuming the relationship of husband and wife, yet, in justice to ourselves and a great principle, we deem it a duty to declare that this act on our part implies no sanction of, nor promise of voluntary obedience to, such of the present laws of marriage as refuse to recognize the wife as an independent rational being, while they confer upon the husband an injurious and unnatural superiority, investing him with legal powers which no honorable man would exercise, and which no man should possess. We protest especially against the laws which give to the husband: —
>
> 1. The custody of the wife's person.
> 2. The exclusive control and guardianship of their children.
> 3. The sole owner of her personal, and use of her real, estate, unless previously settled upon her or placed in the hands of trustees, as is the case of minors, lunatics, and idiots.
> 4. The absolute right to the product of her industry.

5. Also against laws which give to the widower so much larger and more permanent interest in the property of the deceased wife than they give to the widow of the deceased husband.

6. Finally, against the whole system by which the "legal existence of the wife is suspended during marriage," so that in most States she neither has a legal part in the choice of her residence, nor can she make a will, nor sue or be sued in her own name, nor inherit property.

We believe that personal independence and equal human rights can never be forfeited, except for crime; that marriage should be an equal and permanent partnership, and so recognized by law; that until it is so recognized, married partners should provide against the radical injustice of present laws by every means in their power.

We believe that where domestic difficulties arise no appeal should be made to legal tribunals under existing laws, but that all difficulties should be submitted to the equitable adjustment of arbitrators mutually chosen.

Thus reverencing law, we enter protest against rules and customs which are unworthy of the name, since they violate justice, the essence of law.

[Signed]
HENRY B. BLACKWELL.
LUCY STONE.

If all marriages could be entered upon in that spirit, we should be able to realize the truth of Tennyson's great poem, and hasten its fulfilment: as has truly been illustrated in the lives of Lucy Stone and Henry Blackwell: —

"The woman's cause is *man's;* they rise or sink
Together, dwarf'd or godlike, bond or free; . . .
If she be small, slight-natured, miserable,
How shall men grow? . . .
For woman is not undevelopt man,
But diverse. . . .
Yet in the long years, *liker* must they grow;
The man be more of woman, she of man;
He gain in sweetness and in moral height, . . .
She mental breadth, nor fail in childward care,
Nor lose the childlike in the larger mind. . . .
And so these twain, upon the skirts of Time,
Sit side by side, full-summed in all their powers,
. . . .
Self-reverent each, and reverencing each,
Distinct in individualities,
But like each other ev'n as those who love.
Then comes the statelier Eden back to men:
Then reign the world's great bridals, chaste and calm:
Then springs the crowning race of humankind."

This great key-note of Lucy Stone's life, *individuality*, needs striking over and over again, until the dull ears of the cowardly, time-serving multitude of copyists shall be roused to hear it. The world loses more in resources at that point than at any other.

George Eliot has painted for us an exceedingly interesting picture of Stradivarius, the violin-maker of Cremona. We watch the prince of violin-makers as he stands in his workshop, exulting and yet humbled by the marvellous power of his own genius and skill. As he gazes at the beautiful instrument in his hand, he exclaims, —

> "'Tis God gives skill,
> But not without men's hands. He could not make
> Antonio Stradivari's violins
> Without Antonio."

How deep the truth in these words which this queen of novelists puts in the mouth of the old musician! To every one of us is given some genius for supplying the world's need, that is peculiarly our own and is granted to us alone.

Lucy Stone has caught what is the real essence of Christianity in her instant obedience to the command of duty. The sluggish conservative says, "Let the world be as it is;" but the optimistic Christ says, "Make the world what it should be." No man or woman has caught a conception of the true genius of Christianity who admits that a wrong exists, and yet is willing that it should continue, or remains indifferent to its removal. Let us rather

"Strike for that which ought to be,
And God will bless the blows."

That was the spirit in which Lucy Stone lived and died. How fitting that her last words, caught on the ear of her gifted daughter, Alice Stone Blackwell, as she bent over her for the parting message, should have been these so noble, "Make the world better."

Oh, that we all might catch the inspiration of that deathless purpose!

Her work for justice toward woman in the opening of avenues of employment has perhaps met with a readier reward than any other phase of her many-sided life-work. She lived to see the half-dozen employments open to women in her girlhood multiply into hundreds during her serene old age. She was pained, however, in her last years, as we all should be, at the cruel injustice which pays woman to-day not according to the work she performs, but according to her sex.

In Boston the School Board set the example of injustice, and it is followed in all the large stores, so that we have the spectacle of thousands of women, who are expected to pay as much for education, living, travel, and recreation as if they were men, yet constantly discounted from thirty to seventy per cent in their wages because they are women. It is cruelly unjust, and there cannot be other than great sorrow and hardship while it lasts.

She lived long enough to see the great tide of intelligence and opinion set toward the goal for which she labored. She lived to see more than a score of States grant school suffrage to women; to see two others grant them municipal suffrage; and one sovereign State admitted as such by the United States Congress, with equal suffrage impregnably imbedded in its constitution. Although she did not live to see the full fruition of her dreams for humanity, she lived to grasp this token, and in her heart was the faith that all the other States should be fashioned like unto Wyoming.

She lived to see the day when even the most intelligent of her opponents admit that the speedy success of equal privilege and responsibility between the sexes is assured.

The whole current of modern opinion sweeps that way with irresisible force.

Mr. Gladstone said eight years ago, speaking of home rule for Ireland, "You cannot fight against the future." He who fights to sustain the decrepit and dying aristocracy of sex is warring against the future. Woman will come to her own. She will come into the Methodist General Conference and the Presbyterian Synod. She will come to the pulpit and the bar. She will come to the jury-box and the bench. She will come to the ballot, and that will be the golden key to justice in wages, in law, and in society.

Lucy Stone was great in all essential elements. Life to her was always earnest and important. The fires of her consecrated enthusiasm for humanity never burned out — indeed, never burned low.

Many people whose youth has flamed with great and earnest purpose, have lost life's zest in later years, and lived on like a prophet without a message; like extinct volcanoes, interesting only as more or less picturesque ruins of former greatness. But to the end deep earnestness was manifest in whatever Lucy Stone did. That which gave her voice its highest charm was a certain indescribable soul-force with which it was charged. Colonel Higginson, at the funeral service, related how he once took the brilliant Helen Hunt Jackson to hear Lucy Stone speak at a woman-suffrage meeting in New York. On the way she confided to him that she did not in the slightest believe in the claims of the suffragists, that she thought they were the greatest fanatics, but was going to hear them to get the material for an amusing letter for a New York newspaper. Returning home after the meeting, Mr. Higginson said, "Well, I suppose you have plenty of matter for your article?" Seizing his arm with impetuous feeling, she said, "Do you suppose I could write one word against anything that a woman with a voice like Lucy Stone's wanted done?"

Because she gave herself with such sublime consecration to the one great work to which she was as truly called of God as ever prophet or minister was to his mission, some thought she was narrow; but it was the narrowness of the Matterhorn, which contracts the outlines of its lofty cone that it may the better cleave the clouds and mount nearer to the stars; it was the narrowness of the majestic Columbia River, that deepens its channel and gathers its force to cut asunder the Cascade Mountains; it was the narrowness of the thunderbolt, that concentrates its electric might that it may smite that at which it is hurled!

Yet she was broad like the Matterhorn in its wide-reaching base intrenched in the Alps; she was broad like the Columbia, that slakes the thirst of flocks and herds and towns, and makes fertile valleys and plains; she was broad like the electricity, that gives its virile stimulus to the lowliest life. Those who were nearest to her knew that she had great breadth of mind and heart. She was too great for anything narrow or little. She never cherished for a moment a petty feeling of envy or jealousy. In many conversations with her I never detected a note of pique at another's success, which one often grieves over as the infirmity of some good and great people. Lucy Stone rejoiced at the success of every worker for reform, and was always ready with her sympathetic tribute of praise.

She never forgot the lessons learned in the

hard school of poverty and trial; and when fame and consideration and abundance came, she held them all as a steward for any of her brothers and sisters who had need.

That is a characteristic story which Mrs. Livermore tells in the *Transcript:* "I remember on one occasion she was about to take up and help a poor woman for whom I believed little or nothing could be done; a woman I had been through the mill with, and had not succeeded in helping as I wished. I told Lucy Stone all I could tell her. I begged her not to burden herself. She had cares enough already. She heard me through (and I talked, I assure you), and then she said in her soft voice, 'I believe all you say, but I shall do what I intended for her just the same.'"

She had great hospitality for youth. She was never afraid of being crowded to one side. Nothing delighted her more than to see young men and young women enlisting earnestly in the ranks she had so long led.

She lived on a high level of thought and feeling. I never rose from a conversation with her without a sense of having come into touch with a lofty spirit, and going away with something of the stimulus one receives from a view from a hill-top. Lucy Stone lived constantly on the highlands, and breathed always the atmosphere of noble purpose. She grew old retaining her youthful heart and sweetness of spirit. The currents against which she had contended all her life had not soured her. She was young in soul, and courageous to do her duty in all worlds. Mrs. Livermore said at her funeral, " When Lucy Stone celebrated her seventy-fifth birthday, I wrote her a letter. I told her I didn't know whether she would wish to be congratulated or commiserated on being seventy-five. If she felt that it was good, I wished to congratulate her ; and if it seemed too far along the way, and she would rather have commiseration, she should have the commiseration with all my heart, for we were old comrades in the fight, and in every way must keep together in the procession until the end. Her answer was like a bugle-call. She said she would never drop out of the procession. About a fortnight ago I went to see her for the last time, and she held out her hand and repeated some of my words, and said, 'And now I have dropped out.' But the words she added were of perfect fearlessness of death. 'I have always believed it was better farther on,' she said: and when I took her hand before I came away, she said, 'We shall shake hands again sometime, somewhere. We shall know each other and be comrades still.'"

Shall we not all learn her secret of growing old with hands and hearts full of great hopes and deeds, that shall make us able to realize with her the glorious possibilities suggested in Lucy Larcom's sweet poem? —

> "Old — we are growing old:
> Going on through a beautiful road,
> Finding earth a more blessed abode;
> Nobler work by our hands to be wrought,
> Freer paths for our hope and our thought;
> Because of the beauty the years unfold,
> We are cheerfully growing old!
>
> Old — we are growing old:
> Going up where the sunshine is clear;
> Watching grander horizons appear
> Out of the clouds that enveloped our youth;
> Standing firm on the mountains of truth;
> Because of the glory the years unfold,
> We are joyfully growing old!

Old — we are growing old:
Going into the gardens of rest
That glow through the gold of the west,
Where the rose and the amaranth blend,
And each path is the way to a friend;
Because of the peace the years unfold,
We are thankfully growing old

Old — are we growing old?
Life blooms as we travel on
Up to the hills, into fresh, lovely dawn;
We are children who do but begin
The sweetness of living to win;
Because heaven is in us to bud and unfold,
We are younger for growing old!"

XI

FRESH BREAD FOR TO-DAY'S HUNGER

"Give us this day our daily bread."— MATT. vi. 11.

THIS is the appropriate attitude of all men, rich or poor, before God.

It is not the attitude of the worldling who has weaned himself away from his childhood's dependence upon God. You see a good specimen of him in "the rich fool" of the Saviour's parable. Neither is it the attitude of the worrying, fretting soul. Says Amelia E. Barr, " Worrying is just the thing in life that is not needful; for one worry can as effectually spoil its savor as one aching nerve can make the whole body sick. Yet there are undoubtedly self-tormentors, who feel a kind of luxury in having something to worry about, and who even elevate into a virtue their depressing faculty of always being ' prepared for the worst,' though their preparation never in any degree arms them against impending misfortune. However, the troubles that the worrier foresees are seldom real ones. They are only chimeras, with the proportions of giants and the substance of phantoms, yet to the unhappy invokers of them they are at times very real horrors; and when it is 'their hour' a sensible person will not try to fight foes as intangible as ghosts. The paroxysm being on, worriers must be allowed to make themselves as miserable as they desire. Any allusion to the sufferings of others will be set down as indifference to theirs, and an effort to cheer them would be an impertinent doubt of their judgment and foresight: for the true worrier will allow nothing for favorable probabilities, and will suffer nothing to go by faith."

Yet, as she points out, there are more than sixty admonitions in the Bible against fear or unnecessary anxiety, and these so various and yet so positive, that a Christian has not a legitimate subject for worry left. Certainly not on meat and money matters; for he is told, "Behold the fowls of the air: for they sow not, neither do they reap, nor gather into barns; yet your heavenly Father feedeth them. Are ye not much better than they?" Not perplexities and uncertainties; for God has promised, "I will bring the blind by a way that they knew not; I will lead them in paths that they have not known; I will make darkness light before them, and crooked things straight." Not because our work seems greater than our strength; for "He giveth power to the faint; and to them that have no might he increaseth strength." Have we enemies before whom we tremble? "If God be for us, who can be against us?" Are we in sorrow? "I, even I, am he that comforteth you." Do we fear death? Jehovah has promised to strengthen and sustain us, and surely we may smile on that last enemy if God smiles on us!

Our text illustrates the attitude of expectant faith. The richest soul in the universe is the one that completely believes God.

The saintly McCheyne said, "Believe none, and you will have no joy. Believe little, and you will have little joy. Believe much, and you will have much joy. Believe all, and you will have all joy, and your joy will be full. It will be like a bowl lipping over — good measure, pressed down and running over."

The elder Dr. Peabody, surrounded all his life by the doubting class of religionists, assures us that there never was a time when faith was so easy as now, such clear evidence to bear it up. He says, "Pseudo-liberalism has had a long series of what it has deemed final dispensations and undoubtedly destined triumphs. One of the most curious chapters in the history of mind is that of the phases of thought, science, philosophy, speculation, which have been going to put an end to Christianity, but which have themselves come to an early, if not an untimely, end, and which would be forgotten but for obituaries of Christian authorship; and in every instance Christianity has made capital of the bankrupt assets, and has gained wealth and strength from the genius and learning invested for its overthrow. . . . In great part by means of these bankruptcies Christianity stands to-day on a firmer foundation of evidence than ever before. Feeble defences have been broken down, only to reveal their needlessness, only to lay bare the foundation on the Rock of Ages, which they often hid from sight. I hesitate not to say that there are at the present time stronger reasons for believing Christianity and its Author to be the record and incarnation of the divine truth, law, and love, than have been manifest in any preceding age since that when Christ in person bore witness of Himself, and the Father who sent Him bore witness of and with Him."

One well says that "earnest souls know how priceless is this faith which shines through the darkness of sorrow, and feels the helping God ever near, the immortal world bright and sure. There is no loss that can happen to man or woman greater than this — the loss of hope, of confidence in the worth of life, of faith that victory and blessing await those who sincerely seek to know and do the will of God."

There is a touching little poem of a pilgrim band talking together of the great losses that had come to them in life: —

"Some talked of vanished gold,
Some of proud honors told,
Some spoke of friends that were their trust no more."

Some, with quivering lips, spoke of those they had lost in death, and others, with deeper grief, of those they had lost in sin.

> "But, when their tales were done,
>   There spake among them one,
>   A stranger, seeming from all sorrow free:
> 'Sad losses have ye met,
>   But mine is heavier yet;
>   For a believing heart hath gone from me.'
>
> 'Alas,' these pilgrims said,
> 'For the living and the dead,
>   For fortune's cruelty, for love's sure cross,
>   For the wrecks of land and sea, —
> But, however it came to thee,
>   Thine, stranger, is life's last and heaviest loss.'"

And it is true; for experience shows that "all things" in the conquest of sin, the doing of duty, the bearing of trouble — "all things are possible to him that believeth." In the believing heart God and Christ and Love and Heaven are real treasures of which no misfortune can rob us, and which mean strength and courage and eternal hope.

Let us acquaint ourselves with the spirit of the Bible.

A Christian Italian fruit-vender sat behind

her neatly arranged fruit-stand — a girl of fourteen — absorbed in reading her Bible. She did not hear the footsteps of a gentleman who was passing by, and was startled by his question, —

"What are you reading that interests you so much?"

She timidly replied, "The Word of God, sir."

"Who told you that the Bible is the Word of God?" he inquired.

"God told me Himself," she replied, with childlike innocence.

"God told you? Impossible! How did He tell you? You have never seen Him, nor talked with Him. How, then, could He tell you that the Bible is His Word?"

For a few seconds the girl seemed confused and silent. The man, who was a sceptic, and took delight in undermining the faith of people in the Scriptures, felt confident that he had confounded the simple-hearted girl. She soon recovered herself, and her ready wit came to her aid. There was a flash in her dark eyes as she asked, —

"Sir, who told you there is a sun yonder in the blue sky above us?"

"Who told me?" said the man, smiling somewhat contemptuously; for he fancied the girl was trying to hide her ignorance under an irrelevant question. "Who told me? Nobody; I don't need to be told. The sun tells this about itself. It warms me, and I love its light. That is telling enough."

"Sir," cried the girl, with intense earnestness, as she stood before him with clasped hands, "you have put it right for both Bible and sun. That is the way God tells me this is His Book. I read it, and it warms my heart and gives me light. I love its light, and no one but God can give such light and warmth through the pages of a book. It must be His. I don't want more telling; that's telling enough, sir. As sure as the sun is in heaven, so sure is God shining through this Book."

The sceptic was abashed. The earnest faith of the young fruit-seller amazed him. He could adroitly insinuate doubts into the minds of those who have only given intellectual assent to the truth in God's Book, but the girl's heart experience of the power of God's Word was an evidence he could not shake.

If we live in that spirit we shall be able to sing Mrs. Sangster's song. —

> "Give us this day, dear Lord, our daily bread;
>   We do not ask to-morrow's till it come;
> But on the journey, day by day, are fed,
>   Until Thou guide us to our heavenly home.
>
> Give us this day the patience that we need,
>   So many little things our spirits try;
> Give us the Word with eager love to heed,
>   Content, although our wish Thou mayst deny.
>
> Give us this day Thy wisdom: when perplexed
>   We know not how to turn nor what to do;
> Save us, we pray, from being weakly vexed,
>   And lead us, hour by hour, this one day through.
>
> Give us this day the courage and the cheer
>   To face Thy foes and ours with look serene;
> Reveal Thyself, so constant and so near,
>   That we shall see Thee — not a cloud between.
>
> Give us this day more loyalty to Thee,
>   More hatred of the sins that wound Thy heart;
> More grace Thy loving followers to be,
>   Choosing in Thee, for aye, the better part.
>
> Give us this day our own light cross to bear,
>   As though it bore us on to heights divine;
> Give us to realize, Thy cross who share,
>   That still the heaviest end, dear Lord, is Thine.

>   Give us this very day our daily bread;
>   Thou knowest all our wants. That want we bring;
>   And in thy footsteps, Saviour, as we tread,
>   We hail Thee Master and we crown Thee King."

II.

We have here the appropriate attitude toward our fellow-men. Give *us our* daily bread. It is the attitude of brotherhood.

A man could not sincerely pray that prayer, and be at the same time engineering a corner on wheat, or running a sweat-shop, or getting his bread by selling intoxicants, or by renting his property for a saloon or brothel. A man cannot pray that prayer and carry on a chattel-mortgage wreckage shop, or expect to get his bread through a Louisiana lottery ticket, or any of the trickery schemes which are to deprive his neighbor of bread in order to increase the size of his own loaf. Our bread has relation to our neighbor's bread. Give *us* this day *our* daily bread.

I must be sure that in getting my bread I have not poisoned my brother's loaf. I noted a good illustration of this the other day. Lady

Burton was bequeathed by her husband, the late Sir Richard Burton, the manuscript of "The Scented Garden," a collection of very rare but exceedingly immoral tales which he had translated from the Arabic. Lady Burton was offered $30,000 for this manuscript; but, although she had no other property, she preferred to burn it. To a man who assured her that she could easily get fifteen hundred subscribers for the book at twenty dollars each, she answered, "Out of fifteen hundred persons, fifteen would probably read it out of the spirit of science in which it was written, while the other fourteen hundred and eighty-five would read it for filth's sake, then would pass it on to their friends, and the harm done would be incalculable." So she burned the manuscript, showing herself a brave and righteous woman.

That is the spirit of our Lord's Prayer, and it is the spirit that is to transform this wicked world.

The influence of such a character upon the lost is powerfully manifested in the relations of the Bishop with Jean Valjean, the convict, in Victor Hugo's great story. Many of you recall the stream of life and light issuing from the open door and the hospitable welcome and courteous housing of the man who had been a galley convict for twenty-six years, and whose release was but the occasion of a hounding vigilance and suspicion that made freedom an equal slavery with the galleys. There is no stronger description in literature of the struggle of the powers of the good, awakened in the soul by a Christlike touch of kindness, with the powers of evil born and grown in the darkness of social oppression and misery, than the description of Jean Valjean's night in the Bishop's house, when he passes the sleeping Bishop to steal the silver; and the morning scene in the garden, when, in the hands of the officers, the Bishop beholds the thief of the night, and instead of revilings and accusations, adds the silver candlesticks to the silver, explaining that it was a gift, and not a robbery, that had occurred. The power of holy character over men is exhibited with clearness in these words of the Bishop at parting with Jean Valjean, "Jean Valjean, my brother, you no longer belong to evil, but to good. It is your soul that I buy from you. I withdraw it from black thought and the spirit of perdition, and I give it to God." That hour was an apocalypse to the convict. He came forth from it a new creature. Such is the lesson of a godly life.

Brothers, sisters, this is not an impossible ideal that Victor Hugo has drawn — it is a transcript of that high and holy command, "As the Father hath sent me, even so send I you."

In New York city, during one of the blisteringly hot nights of a recent summer, a minister was tossing on his bed in his comfortable room. No such high temperature for twenty years. His sleep was troubled. The whole city round about was feverish. He was dreaming wretchedly of the suffering children seeking rest upon the roofs, doorsteps, pavements, wagons standing in the streets — everywhere out of the houses. The windows were open: it was two o'clock. In his sleep he heard a faint little cry, the call of a tiny and feeble infant. Any father, sleeping never so soundly, would have aroused instantly. Out on the sidewalk a man was walking back and forth carrying a child. It was the work of a few moments to reach him.

"Its mother is worn out; I am doing what I can; I am afraid we can't keep her. I work all day. This is my *seventh night of it.*" The little one was soon stretched upon a suitable pillow. It had cooling and refreshing drink. The father, with unspeakable gratitude, lay down upon the sidewalk and slept. The minister walked with the child till long after daylight.

Do you think it would be very hard to make that man believe in Christianity after that? If we illustrate Christianity in a living, breathing brotherhood they can apprehend it.

One of the most influential characters in England just now is Mr. Ben Tillett, a day-laborer in the east of London, and a member of a Congregational Church in that quarter. He was one of the leaders of the dock laborers' strike a few years ago. During that time he was one day addressing a crowd of dockmen, and knowing how that crowd hates a sermon, but also how warm are their hearts, he went on to describe, with great power and pathos, the Man of Nazareth. He gave the every-day history of the Master, and told what he thought

He would do if He owned the docks. The crowd stood, hushed and attentive, till he had finished; when one big, grimy fellow shouted, "Ben Tillett, I don't know who this Man of Nazareth is that you've been talking about, but I move we give Him three cheers"—and cheers rang out from thousands of throats of men who had dimly recognized the Son of God.

God help us to win appreciation for our Lord by the brotherly attitude of our daily lives!

XII

A GLAD SIGHT FOR WEARY EYES

"Sir, we would see Jesus." — JOHN xii. 21.

THIS was the language of a little company of Greeks. The Greeks were the most like modern peoples of all those who lived in the days of Christ. They were a bright, alert sort of people; always digging into the whys and wherefores of things, and ready to pounce on a new idea as a hawk seizes on a bird. Any man with a bright thought was sure of a hearing and a debate among the Grecians. These restless, inquisitive Greeks came over to Jerusalem from some city like Corinth or Ephesus; and immediately on arrival they heard conversation on every hand about Jesus. It was the chief subject of discussion everywhere. In the inn, in the bazaar, along the street, as well as about the temple door, people were talking earnestly about Jesus. They were discussing, no doubt, the singular gentleness of His manner, His strange, revolutionary addresses, and the marvellous miracles which He performed. The Greek travellers, on hearing this, are fired with interest, and immediately try to find some one who can give them an introduction to Jesus. Some one of whom they make inquiry refers them to Philip, doubtless because he has the reputation of being a friend of Christ's. Blessed reputation! My brother, you may see here one of the chief duties of a Christian — to introduce strangers to Jesus.

Now, I have called your attention to this incident that we might reflect on the beauty and profit of beholding Jesus. There are several ways in which we may see Jesus, all of them different, and each of them important. I can only enumerate some of the chief offices in which we may behold Jesus as the great Leader and Burden-bearer of our race.

I.

We may see Jesus as a Teacher. Jesus is the great teacher of mankind in spiritual things.

How infinitely superior He is we do not appreciate until we compare the bright sunlight of His words with the vague uncertainty of the utterances of the greatest teachers and philosophers the world has known.

Phillips Brooks, in his lecture on "The Influence of Jesus on the Intellectual Life of Man," draws a striking parallel between the teaching of Socrates and Jesus concerning the mysteries of death and the future life. The philosopher asks, "Shall a man who really loves knowledge, and who is firmly persuaded that he shall never truly attain it except in Hades, be angry and sorry to have to die?" The Son of God says, "Now I go to him that sent me." Socrates says, "Be well assured I do expect this, that I shall be among good men, though this I do not feel so confident about; but I shall go to gods who are good governors." Jesus cries, "Now, O Father, glorify thou me with thine own self." Socrates draws in confused but elaborate detail the road to Hades and its geography. Jesus says, "In my Father's house are many mansions;" and, "Father, I will that they whom thou hast given me be with me where I am." Socrates is noble in his frank uncertainty about life. He says, "Whether I tried in the right way, and with what success, I shall know certainly when I arrive there, if it please God." Jesus is divine in His certainty: "O righteous Father, the world hath not known thee, but I have known thee." And again, "I have finished the work which thou gavest me to do." Socrates tells of a "demon" or angel who has the care of every man while he is alive, and when he is dead takes him to the place of judgment. Jesus says, "I will pray the Father, and he shall give you another Comforter, that he may abide with you forever." "He shall testify of me." Socrates says when they ask him for his last legacy, "If you take good care of yourself you will always gratify me and mine most." Jesus says, "This is my commandment, That ye love one another, as I have loved you."

How immeasurably above the enlightened selfishness or the guesses of the philosophers is the sublime teaching of Jesus! Shall we not sit at His feet and be His disciples?

II.

We may see Jesus as a Redeemer. The dark pall of sin is over all the earth. Sin has crippled and baffled every man that has sought to master it in his own strength. When once a man has done a wrong thing it has an awful power of attracting him and making him hunger to do it again. If the wall of a dyke is sound it will keep the water out, but it is useless when once the tiniest breach has been made; the trickling rill soon becomes the flood. So the course of evil is ever wider and deeper and more tumultuous. Some one says, "The little sins get in at the window, and open the front door for the big housebreakers." One smooths the path for the other. All sin has an awful power of perpetuating and increasing itself. As the prophet says in his terrible vision of the doleful creatures that make sport in the desolate city, "None of them shall want her mate. The wild beasts of the desert shall meet with the wild beasts of the islands." Every sin tells upon the character, and makes the repetition of itself more and more easy. "None is barren among them." And all sin is linked together in a slimy tangle, like a field of seaweeds, so that the swimmer, once caught in its oozy fingers, is almost sure to drown.

It was into a world so held in bondage that Jesus came as a Redeemer.

Some years ago a war raged in India between the English and a native monarch named Tippoo Sahib. On one occasion several English officers were taken prisoners; among them one named Baird. One day a native officer brought in fetters to be put on each of the prisoners, the wounded not excepted. Baird had been severely wounded, and was suffering from pain and weakness. A gray-haired officer said to the native official, —

"You do not think of putting chains upon that wounded young man?"

"There are just as many pairs of fetters as there are captives," was the answer, "and every pair must be worn."

"Then," said the officer, "put two pairs on me. I will wear his as well as my own."

The end of the story is that Baird lived to regain his freedom — lived, indeed, to take captive that very city; but the generous friend died in prison. He wore two pairs of fetters. But what if he had worn the fetters for all in the prison? What if, instead of being a captive himself, he had been free and great, and had quitted a glorious palace to live in their loathsome dungeon, to wear their chains, to bear their stripes, to suffer and die in their stead, that they might go free? Yet that is what Jesus has done. It is my blessed privilege to tell you, here and now, that no matter how black the pall of sin may hang over you, no matter how painful and disgraceful the handcuffs of sin may be that hold you in bondage, if you will receive the free grace of God's Son your chains shall be stricken off, and your prison doors be thrown wide open.

III

We may see Jesus as the Captain, not only of our own salvation, but of the spiritual armies that are battling for righteousness among men. The mission of Jesus in the world is to make a glorious conquest. Each one of us who are

His followers is called to be a soldier in a stern conflict. You and I have to take our turn not only on the battle-field, but also in the more trying duty of standing "on guard." Our Captain has left special orders for us to "watch."

A general, after gaining a great victory, was encamping with his army for the night. He ordered sentinels to be stationed all around the camp as usual. One of the sentinels, as he went to his station, grumbled to himself, and said, "Why could not the general let us have a quiet night's rest for once, after beating the enemy? I am sure there is nothing to be afraid of." The man then went to his station, and stood for some time looking about him. It was a bright summer night, but he could see nothing anywhere; so he said, "I am terribly tired; I shall sleep for just five minutes, out of the moonlight, under the shadow of this tree." So he lay down. Presently he started up, dreaming that some one had pushed a lantern before his eyes; and he found that the moon was shining brightly down on him through a hole in the branches of the tree above him.

The next minute an arrow whizzed past his ears, and the whole field before him seemed alive with soldiers in dark green coats, who sprang up from the ground, where they had been silently creeping onward, and rushed toward him. Fortunately the arrow had missed him; so he shouted aloud to give the alarm, as he ran back to some other sentinels. The army was thus saved; but the soldier said, "I shall never forget as long as I live that when one is at war one must watch."

Napoleon one night set his pickets thick on the outposts of the camp. The order was, "Let nothing pass." The night wore on, and nothing sought to pass that line of trusty sentinels. At last, in that deep darkness which precedes the dawn, a great dog came near the picket guard. "Back, sir, back!" cried the soldier. The dog whined and fawned, then moved past the line toward the sleeping tents. Another moment and the poor animal fell dead; the sentry and his gun had been faithful to the commander's orders. Now the long lines of pickets are alert and stirring, the great camp is aroused, and the chief sends out a detachment to learn the cause of the single shot that had thrilled each heart in that great army. "Only a dog. Why, 'tis the captain's missing dog! Poor fellow, he has been gone for weeks, and now has come home only to die," said a soldier. But look more nearly; off with the hide! 'tis a man, a slight fellow, in the missing dog's coat. "So perish all spies!" say they, while the faithful sentry, whose heart had so rebelled against shooting an innocent dog, and obeying so rigid and seemingly foolish an order, went back to his post full of grave thoughts concerning duty and obedience — that first great law which every soldier must learn.

Our whole life is a war with evil, and even when we are most watchful many a stray dog of sin will seek to skulk into our camp. Our Captain says to us. "Watch and pray, that ye enter not into temptation." Sometimes great interests depend upon our fortitude and faithfulness.

A little while ago, on the occasion of the death of General Corse, I was interested in reading again the incident which gave rise to the popular gospel song "Hold the Fort," as it is given by the historian Lossing: At a place called Altoona a great quantity of stores belonging to the government had been left by General Sherman, defended only by a small company. Suddenly the General found that the enemy had marched in heavy force toward this point with the purpose of capturing the garrison and the large amount of stores. He immediately despatched relief. From the summit of Kenesaw, General Sherman could see the smoke and hear the booming of the great guns at Altoona, although eighteen miles distant.

With signal flags, on the summit of the great Kenesaw Mountain, which were seen through the field-glasses, he called to the commander at Altoona, "Hold the fort; for relief is coming!"

To the great delight of Sherman, an answer came back from General Corse, —

"I will!"

"He will hold out: I know the man!" exclaimed Sherman to an officer standing near him.

How is it with you, my brother, in regard to the work the Captain has set you to do — the fortress of truth and righteousness He has set you to defend? Have you been so faithful that the Captain of your salvation can turn to the angel that stands by His side, and say, "He will hold out, I know; for I know the man?"

IV

We may see Jesus as a Friend. "I call you not servants; I have called you friends," is the sweetest thing that Jesus ever said to His disciples. And no other friend is so tender and loving as Christ. There is a marvellous power in a sincere, sympathetic friendship to soothe a weary heart.

There is a story told in connection with our war of a mother who received a despatch that her boy was mortally wounded. She immediately went down to the front; for she knew that the soldiers told off to watch the sick and wounded could not watch her boy as she could. So she went to the doctor, and said, —

"Would you let me take care of my boy?"

The doctor said, —

"He has just gone to sleep, and if you go to

him the surprise will be so great it may be dangerous to him. He is in a very critical state. I will break the news to him gradually."

"But," said the mother, "he may never wake up; I should so dearly like to see him!"

Oh, how she longed to see him!

Finally the doctor said,

"Well, you can see him; but if you wake him up and he dies it will be your fault."

"I will not wake him up," she said, "if I may only go by his dying cot and see him."

She went to the side of the cot. Her eyes had longed to see him; and as she gazed upon him she could not keep her hand off that pallid forehead, and she laid it gently there. There was love and sympathy in her touch, and the moment the slumbering boy felt it, he said, —

"O mother, have you come?"

He knew there was sympathy and affection in the touch of that hand. And it brought more speedy healing to him than all the doctors and their medicine.

And if you, my brother, who have been indifferent or sinful, will but let Jesus reach out His hand and touch your heart, you, too, will find that there is sympathy and love and healing in the Saviour's touch.

And this friendship with Jesus will not be sundered by death. Indeed, we are persuaded that no true friendship between pure souls can be affected by death. It will comfort you to read over, with this thought in your mind, the history of Jesus' communion with His friends after His death and resurrection. Behold the risen Christ! He has been crucified upon the cross; He has been buried for three days in Joseph's tomb — but now that He has burst the bands of death no change has come over His mind, His memory, or His heart. His thoughts all flow in the same old channels. There is the same heavenly tone in His words; He lingers in the same favorite places; He seeks the same society of His disciples. Their names are as dear to Him as of yore; and we hear Him saying, "Simon, lovest thou me?" or speaking softly, "Mary!"

The new life is but the old life on a higher, holier level — the old life transfigured, with all its earthiness removed. Death only gathers up the broken links of life and welds them together for eternity. We sometimes speak of our friends who have gone on before us as "lost." They are not lost. They are ours still, ours as much as they ever were; and they will be ours forever.

Whittier sings, —

> " I have friends in the spirit land;
> Not shadows in a shadowy band —
> Not others, but themselves, are they;
> And still I think of them the same
> As when the Master's summons came."

Earth is only the beginning of that perfect friendship which shall find its full fruition in the heavenly home on high. We are only pilgrims here.

In recent years some most interesting experiments have been made with homing pigeons as messengers. One is lost in admiration at the fidelity of these birds to their home, and the mysterious faculty by which they find their way. Loose the homing pigeon anywhere, and it starts instantly homeward. If you carry it far away and toss it up, it spirals to a great height in the air, sails around a moment or two, chooses its course, and sets out for home, making sometimes a hundred miles an hour and a flight a thousand miles long. This knowledge is strange enough to fill us with awe. It is as if that little flying craft of the upper ocean, with trim, slender hull and wide spread of canvas, had machinery on board for winding in its clue, as the Great Eastern might take upon board and coil away an Atlantic cable from mid-ocean shoreward, so coming in at last to the headlands of Heart's Content.

> " ' Oh, wise little birds, how do ye know
> The way to go?'
> 'We but obey
> One who calleth us far away,
> And maketh the way appear.' "

Heinrich Heine, having passed through scepticism of the bitterest sort, at last came to be a Christian. He attributed his conversion to reading the Bible, and declared that, as he read it, "a sort of heavenly homesickness fell upon me and drove me forth."

The homing instinct is in the soul of man; and the God who placed such marvellous faculty of finding its way in the little pigeon's brain, has not left the human heart without chart or compass. We circle around like pigeons, bewildered, in the air, till we take the way of Christ homeward through penitence, forgiveness, and obedience; and as we settle down to our steady flight heavenward, we sing, —

> "This is the way I long have sought,
> And mourned because I found it not."

XIII

OUR BROTHER IN YELLOW

AMERICA'S VISION FROM THE HOUSETOP; OR, THE CHINESE IN THE SHEET OF MODERN CIVILIZATION.

"What God hath cleansed, make not thou common."— ACTS x. 15 (R. V.).

IN America to-day we are looking on a vision like Peter's. The panorama is on a grander scale. Instead of from a tanner's house in Joppa, we look from the vantage-ground of nearly nineteen centuries of toilsome climb. For a sheet we have the world-wide folds of modern civilization; and inside, not "four-footed beasts and creeping things," but "all sorts and conditions of men." The message, however, is the same — that "God is no respecter of persons," but "hath made of one blood all nations of men for to dwell on all the face of the earth."

That the vision might be indelibly stamped on Peter's memory, it was three times repeated before his astonished gaze. The American people are for the third time, as a nation, confronted with this great vision and its divine message of equality and brotherhood. It first came to us to show us our duty to the black man. Keen-eyed souls like Garrison and Phillips and Whittier and Lowell — the Peters of that later day — caught the message by intuition. In those shrewd "Biglow Papers" Lowell sings what it took a baptism of fire and blood to teach the multitude, —

> " Laborin' man an' laborin' woman
> Hev one glory an' one shame.
>
> 'Tain't by turnin' out to hack folks
> You're a-goin' to git your right,
> Nor by lookin' down on black folks
> Coz you're put upon by wite.
>
> Slavery ain't o' nary color,
> 'Tain't the hide that makes it wus,
> All it keers fer in a feller
> 'S jest to make him fill its pus."

Wendell Phillips tells us that when Daniel O'Connell entered the British Parliament with

Ireland on his heart, there were only two members there to speak for the antislavery cause, — Lushington and Buxton. These two had an agreement with each other that when Lushington spoke Buxton cheered him, and when Buxton spoke Lushington cheered him, and those were the only cheers they ever got. When O'Connell came into Parliament, what was known as the slave party, or faction, went to him with the proposition that if he would never go with those Abolitionists they would give him twenty-seven votes solid on every Irish question; but threatened that if he voted with the Abolitionists they would be always solid against him. Grandly did O'Connell stand the test. "Gentlemen," said he, "God knows I speak for the saddest people the sun sees; but may my right hand forget its cunning, and my tongue cleave to the roof of my mouth, if to save Ireland — even Ireland — I forget the negro one single hour." Years afterward the same grand hero in the midst of a great speech lifted from the table a thousand-pound note, sent from New Orleans to help the Irish cause. He came to the front of the platform and said, "This is a draft of one thousand pounds from the slaveholders of New Orleans, the unpaid wages of the negro. Mr. Treasurer, I suppose the treasury is empty?" The treasurer nodded, and O'Connell went on, "Old Ireland is very poor; but, thank God, she is not poor enough to take the unpaid wages of anybody. Send it back!" Phillips well says of him, "The ocean of his philanthropy knew no shore."

And is not that the message of Peter's vision at Joppa — that there are to be no shore-lines to our philanthropy, but that all men are our brothers?

The Rev. Hugh Price Hughes of London has been studying the splendid utterances of Joseph Mazzini, the Christian hero and patriot of Italy, and comes to the conclusion that "Democracy is hell let loose, unless it is the democracy of Mazzini, democracy founded upon God." The democracy of Mazzini, like that of Jesus Christ, has for its corner-stone "The Solidarity of Mankind." Listen to the beautiful and eloquent words in which Mazzini himself expresses this great Christian truth, —

"Foremost and grandest amid the teachings

of Christ were these two inseparable truths — *There is but one God; all men are the sons of God;* and the promulgation of these two truths changed the face of the world, and enlarged the moral circle to the confines of the inhabited globe. To the duties of men towards the family and country were added duties towards humanity. Man then learned that wheresoever there existed a human being there existed a brother; a brother with a soul immortal as his own, destined like himself to ascend towards the Creator, and on whom he was bound to bestow love, a knowledge of the faith, and help and counsel when needed."

As Mazzini says in this remarkable passage, the love of home had existed from the beginning. So had the love of fatherland. Patriotism was found in the Greek and in the Roman heart as well as in the Christian; but the love of the whole human race — that was a new idea. "That sentiment," says Mr. Hughes, "was a distinct addition to the moral stock of humanity." As the great German philologist, Max Müller, says, the very word "humanity" never existed on earth until Christ came. It was then for the first time created to express a new conception. To use the beautiful language of Mazzini, "The chord of humanity was mute upon the Greek lyre." This is Christianity's great message — "There is but one God; all men are the sons of God."

Only a little while ago Helen Hunt Jackson called us to a halt in regard to our dealings with "Our Brother in Red," and by her heartbreaking revelations of "A Century of Dishonor," brought the blush of shame to every true American cheek. And now it is the little Yellow Man from the East who is in our vision, and whose brotherhood demands our recognition.

During the past week the Supreme Court of the United States has rendered a decision, by a vote of five to three, as important from a moral standpoint as the infamous Dred-Scott decision. I refer to the decision declaring constitutional what is known as the "Geary Act," relating to Chinese registration.

This Act is certainly the climax of infamous legislation in our relations with China. It deliberately and with brutal frankness violates our plighted faith as recorded in a treaty which emanated from us, and which we earnestly entreated the Chinese to sign against their desire. This is the way that treaty reads: "The United States of America and the Emperor of China cordially recognize the inherent and unalienable right of man to change his home and allegiance, and also the mutual advantage of free migration and emigration of their citizens and subjects respectively from one country to the other, for the purpose of curiosity, of trade, or as permanent residents." With curious folly this Act proposes to break the treaty wherever it pleases us, by the most insulting restrictions, and hold it in good force wherever it provides for the protection of American citizens. The conditions of the Act are such that in a majority of cases it cannot possibly be obeyed. Every Chinaman is required to prove by a *white* witness that he has been in this country during the whole time of Chinese restrictive legislation, reaching back to the administration of President Hayes. Many of these people cannot speak or understand our language. They are not a fixed population, and are often obliged to cross the continent in pursuit of work, putting them out of the reach of witnesses, if such exist.

Representative Hitt, of Illinois, in his speech in Congress when the bill was under discussion, said: "The rule of all free countries and all civil laws is reversed. . . . Every one can understand how difficult, how almost impossible, it is to make out such a long and costly line of proof, especially to a laboring man. This he must prove affirmatively or he can get no certificate. If he is not granted a certificate — and we can readily see how officers on the Pacific coast would be glad to refuse it — he is arrested, imprisoned six months or less, and then expelled from the country. If he obtains it, he must carry it around with him, or be liable instantly and always to arrest, imprisonment, and deportation, like a convict. It is proposed to have one hundred thousand, or, as some gentlemen assert, two hundred thousand, men in our country ticketed, tagged, almost branded — the old slavery days returned. Never before in a free country was there such a system of tagging a man like a dog, to be caught by the police and examined; and, if his tag or collar is not all right, taken to the pound, or drowned, or shot."

Both Justice Brewer and Justice Field point out clearly, in their dissent from the decision of a majority of the Supreme Court, that if such a law as this can be sustained there is no guaranty that similar treatment may not be accorded to other classes of our population than the Chinese. Justice Field, who has himself resided in California for many years, and who stands without a superior as a fearless man and able jurist, says in the course of his remarks, —

"Aliens domiciled within the country by its consent are entitled to all the guaranties for the protection of their person and property which are secured to native-born citizens. The moment any human being comes within the jurisdiction of the United States, with the consent of the government — and such consent will always be implied when not expressly withheld, and in the case of the Chinese laborers before us was in terms given by treaty — he becomes subject to all their laws and amenable to their punishment and entitled to their protection. Arbitrary and despotic authority can no more be exercised over them with reference to their persons and property than over the persons and property of native-born citizens. They differ only from citizens in the respect that they cannot vote or hold any public office. As men having our common humanity they are protected by all the guaranties of the Constitution. To hold that they are subject to any different law, or are less protected in any particular, is, in my judgment, against the teachings of our history, the practice of our government, and the language of our Constitution.

"Let us test this doctrine by a few illustrations: If a foreigner, who resides in the country by its consent, commits a public offence, is he subject to be cut down, maltreated, imprisoned, or put to death by violence, without accusation made, trial had, and judgment of an established tribunal following the regular forms of judicial procedure? If any rule in the administration of justice is to be omitted or discarded in his case, what rule is to be? If one rule may be laid aside in his case, another rule may be laid aside, and all rules may be so treated. In such instances a rule of evidence may be set aside in one case, a rule of pleading in another. The testimony of eye-witnesses may be rejected and hearsay adopted, or no evidence at all may be received, but simply an inspection of the accused, as is often the case in tribunals of Asiatic countries where personal caprice and not settled rules prevail. That would be to establish a pure, simple, undisguised despotism and tyranny with respect to them and their class; and such an exercise of power is not permissible under our Constitution.

"I utterly dissent from and reject the doctrine and opinion of the majority that Congress might have directed any Chinese laborer found within the United States without a certificate of residence to be removed out of the country by executive officers, without judicial trial or examination, just as it might have authorized such officers absolutely to prevent their entrance into the country. An arrest for that purpose could not be a reasonable seizure of the person within the meaning of the fourth article of the amendment to the Constitution. It would be brutal and oppressive. The existence of the power thus stated is only consistent with the admission that the government is one of unlimited and despotic power so far as aliens domiciled in the country are concerned. According to its theory, Congress might have ordered executive officers to take the Chinese laborers to the ocean and put them into a boat and set them adrift, or might have ordered executive officers to take them to the borders of Mexico and turn them loose there, and in both cases without any means of support; indeed, it might have sanctioned toward these laborers the most shocking brutality conceivable. I utterly repudiate all such notions, and reply that brutality, inhumanity, or cruelty are not elements in any procedure for the enforcement of any laws of the United States. Had the punishment been a fine, or anything else than of an infamous character, it might have been imposed without an indictment; but not so now, unless we hold that a foreigner, though domiciled by the consent of the government of the country, is withdrawn from all the guaranties of due process of law prescribed by the Constitution when charged with an offence to which the grave punishment designated is affixed. The punishment is beyond all reason in its severity. It is out of all proportion to the alleged offence. It is cruel and unusual. As to its cruelty, nothing can exceed a forcible deportation from a country of one's residence and the breaking up of all the relations of friendship, family, and business there contracted.

"I will pursue the subject no farther. The decision of the court and the sanction it would give to legislation depriving resident aliens of the guaranties of the Constitution fill me with apprehensions. These guaranties are of priceless value to every one resident in the country, whether citizen or alien. I cannot but regard the decision as a blow against constitutional liberty when it declares that Congress has the right to disregard the guaranties of the Constitution intended for all men domiciled in the country, with the consent of the government, in their rights of person and property.

"How far will this legislation go? The unnaturalized citizen feels it to-day; but if Congress can disregard the guaranties with respect to any resident of the country, with the consent of the government, it may disregard the guaranties with respect to naturalized citizens. What assurance have we that it may not declare that naturalized citizens of a particular country cannot remain in the United States after a certain day unless they have in their possession a certificate that they are of good moral character and attached to the principles of our Constitution, which certificate they must obtain from a collector of internal revenue, upon the testimony of at least one competent witness of a nationality to be designated by the government? What answer could the naturalized citizen in that case make which cannot be urged in behalf of the poor and despised Chinese laborers of to-day?"

This must make a very interesting question to some who have been very ardent in their persecution of the Chinese. When once we get into the habit of violating our national pledges, who can tell where we will stop? Whose turn shall come next — the Italian? the German? or the Irish? A crusade born of religious or political prejudice may make the position of any class unsafe at any time, when once we have entered on the discord and chaos of a career of injustice. Theodore Parker well says, "Justice is the key-note of the world, and all else is ever out of tune." And John Boyle O'Reilly truly sings, with the same thought in mind, —

> "Wherever a principle dies —
> Nay, principles never die!
> But wherever a ruler lies,
> And a people share the lie;
>
> Where right is crushed by force,
> And manhood is stricken dead —
> There dwelleth the ancient curse,
> And the blood on the earth is red!"

One of the most deplorable features of the whole matter, aside from the direct dishonor of such action, is that no intelligent man believes for a moment that such a bill could have been passed on its merits; but that members of Congress of both parties permitted themselves to be made the tools of an infamous race prejudice, because it was understood that the electoral vote of the Pacific-coast States, on the last presidential election, would be affected by it. I was born on the Pacific coast, and lived there for thirty years, was there through the riots of six and seven years ago; and I say deliberately that there was no just cause for the cruel persecution the Chinese received. It was not a question of low wages through Chinese competition; for during those years the highest wages paid to workingmen in the civilized world were being paid on the Pacific coast.

Several reasons contributed to that agitation; first of all, that race prejudice which bound the black man in slavery and reddened every frontier with Indian wars. Another reason was that the Chinese as a class do not drink and were of no value to the saloon, that infamous fortress of political misrule. Again, they had no vote, and a disfranchised class always suffers. Women are not on an equality with men before the eyes of the law, even in Massachusetts, for the same reason.

The result of the enforcement of this law will be to make America a hermit nation, as Korea has been, in relation to the most populous nation in the world. It is an international confession that our plighted honor is not worth the paper it is written on.

What illustrations America is giving the world in these days of the light feeling of responsibility we have about making good our promises! Only this week it is announced that the Directory of the World's Fair at Chicago have by a large majority voted to open the Exposition on Sunday, despite the fact that they have already received nearly two millions of dollars on the express condition that they would not open on Sunday, and after millions of dollars have been invested in the enterprise from all parts of the civilized world with the same understanding. If these men were to so act in regard to their private business affairs, they would be voted dishonest and unprincipled scoundrels by every newspaper and every sane man in the land. Why is the same action in a representative capacity worthy of more charitable judgment? And yet this World's Fair Directory are only following in the footsteps of the Congress and President of the United States, who united in the passage of the Chinese Registration Act, in open violation of our treaty with China.

It is not flattering to our national pride, but

it is certainly pertinent to the situation, to ask, in all seriousness, if we are coming to be a nation of liars!

What cutting reproof is couched in the following quotations from a Chinese newspaper! The *Shun pao*, published in Shanghai, says, "What is a treaty of peace but that two countries are to be at peace? If they in their intercourse with each other act fairly, they are at peace; but if either should be partial, then there would be unfairness, and unfairness leads to a cessation of peace." After quoting the eleventh article of the American-Chinese treaty of 1844, and the sixth of the Burlingame treaty of 1868, it goes on: "From these it may be seen that Americans are to treat the Chinese in the same manner as the Chinese the Americans. Now, suppose China were to expel the Americans, or to prevent their coming; would Congress allow it to be done? It is indeed true that the Chinese in America sometimes commit crimes; but if such are to be deported, what of the Westerners in China who commit crimes? And there have been surely such. In these instances in the past we only petitioned their judges to try them; and though they have generally gone on the principle that 'punishment ought to be light where there is any doubt of guilt,' and punished the offenders lightly when evidence was (to us) convincing, we never interfered with their judgment. . . . We see from this bill that America is bent upon breaking every intercourse with China, and on abrogating the treaties. . . . She thus presumes on her might, and ill-treats the Chinese laborers, who are but men of toil and without influence or power. She has that quality which causes men to tyrannize over the weak and to fear the strong. Does she not herself feel degraded? . . . It is known that the Chinese helped to open and develop their country, and now they who were benefited by their labors have thus requited them. Is it in this manner that 'America is to treat the Chinese according as she treats the most favored nation'? She indeed can treat us with impunity, but as to how she is to face the world, and with what countenance her citizens can quietly reside in our country, we do not wish to discuss."

Nothing could be more mortifying and unfortunate than the position in which this Act puts the missionaries of all Christian denominations in China. They have been preaching to the people "Thou shalt not lie!" and yet our government deliberately falsifies itself in relation to a most solemn treaty. They have been urging upon them the transforming power of Christian faith; and now the land from which the missionaries come treats the Chinese in a way aptly described by Congressman Hitt as a "revival of the darkest features of the darkest ages in the history of man."

This legislation does not represent Christianity, and it does not fairly represent the average citizenship of this country. It represents the narrow-minded and vicious elements of the Pacific-coast population, who are given power to work this disgrace because of the shameless cowardice of political leaders in all parties.

It is surely a time when Christians and patriots who value the honor of their country should speak out, and let it be known that there is another current of public sentiment in this country — a current that is not swayed by the beer-saloon or the "sand-lot." The outspoken indignation of Christians throughout the country will arouse such a ground-swell of public sentiment that Congress will be compelled to repeal this infamous law. In no other way can the work of our missionaries, accomplished through many long and weary years, be saved from disaster, our commerce with China preserved from annihilation, and our good name protected from ineffaceable shame.

Let every Christian be counted for justice toward " Our Brother in Yellow "!

XIV

THE PROBLEM OF MAN-FLIGHT

"They that wait upon the Lord shall renew their strength; they shall mount up with wings as eagles." — ISA. xl. 31.

A FEW weeks ago the postman laid upon my table a little volume entitled "The Problem of Man-flight." I opened it curiously, and found it to be a brief summary of the efforts of mankind in aerial navigation. As I looked it over, I thought of all the checkered career of the persistent effort of man, by aid of balloon and flying-machine, to navigate the air. I thought of John Müller and his artificial eagle; of the war balloons in the siege of Paris; of the parachutes and the silly victims of the county fairs; of Darius Green and his flying-machine; of all the hodge-podge of wise and unwise efforts of our race to imitate the winged creatures of the air. But as I pondered my meditation took a more serious mood, and I said to myself, After all, this desire to fly must be a very deep and permanent characteristic of the soul. No amount of failure is able to permanently put it down or disappoint it. And, whatever may be the future success of the navigation of the air by the human body, there can be no doubt that a much more important flight of the soul is possible to us every one.

We have in this noble passage of Isaiah the very simple conditions by which the soul may obtain wings and mount up to a noble career. If there is in your heart a sense of revolt against narrow limitations, and a longing for wider vision and nobler achievement, let us study sincerely the conditions of a buoyant, soaring life; for we may be sure that no great life will ever result from anything less than honest preparation for it. So much of any great, successful achievement is hidden away out of sight, that many people, who envy the triumph of great souls and covet their success, do not dream of the hard toil, the tremendous self-denial, and the supreme devotion out of which the victory which they covet was born.

How few people, seeing the splendid ocean steamer sailing out of New York Harbor, think of the great coal-bins down underneath the water in the ship's heart, and the scores of sweating workers feeding its hidden fires, from which comes its splendid speed. On the City of Paris there are sixty firemen, who feed the fiery maws of the forty-five furnaces that create steam in nine boilers. Fifty coal-passers shovel fuel from the bunkers to the furnace door, where the firemen toss it in. And there is something more than the mere shovelling of coal in firing: the stoker must know how to put on the coals so that they will not burn too quickly nor deaden the fire; and he must know how to stir or poke the fire so as to get all the heat out of the coal. These grimy workers, hidden away out of sight in the ship's hold, shovel into the furnaces fifteen tons of coal every hour, or three hundred and sixty tons a day. And yet many people cross the ocean without thinking of that little world underneath them, whose toilers, by their unresting activity, render it possible for the ship to make the passage in a single week.

Let this lead us to think how important it is that we wisely feed the fires of the soul, that it may make rapid and glorious flights across life's stormy sea.

The first great condition that is laid down for us is that of waiting on the Lord. They that wait on the Lord shall fly. He that prays in secret is rewarded openly. Joseph's prayers in the dungeon in Egypt were rewarded on its throne. Daniel and his friends, praying in their secret chamber together, found reward in wide opportunity for influence and blessing. There is no kind of prayer needed so much in our age as secret prayer. There is no art that is in such danger of being lost as the art of meditation. This nervous, restless, inventive time of ours, with its rapid travel, its noise and bustle, threatens to rob men of the old habit of solitary meditation and communion with their own souls and with God. Yet nothing can take the place of that sincere, reverent waiting upon the Lord. David said that when he was in trouble the Lord would hide him in His pavilion, in the secret of His tabernacle, and would shut him in from the strife of tongues; and so you and I need, every one of us, daily to have some time when we are shut in with God and protected, for a while at least, from the strife of tongues. Father Ryan's old poem about the valley of silence tells it most helpfully. —

> "I walk down the valley of silence,
>   Down the dim, voiceless valley alone;
> And I hear not the fall of a footstep
>   Around me, save God's and my own;
> And the hush of my heart is as holy
>   As hovers where angels have flown.
>
> Long ago I was weary of voices
>   Whose music my heart could not win;
> Long ago I was weary of noises
>   That fretted my soul with their din;
> Long ago I was weary of places
>   Where I met but the human and sin.
>
> I walked through the world with the worldly,
>   Yet I craved what the world never gave;
> And I said, 'In the world each ideal
>   That shines like a star on life's wave
> Is tossed on the shores of the real,
>   And sleeps like a dream in a grave.'
>
> And still did I pine for the perfect,
>   And still found the false with the true;
> And sought 'mid the human for heaven,
>   But caught a mere glimpse of its blue;

And I wept when the clouds of the mortal
　Veiled even that glimpse from my view.

And I toiled on, heart-tired of the human,
　And I mourned 'mid the mazes of men;
Till I knelt, long ago, at an altar,
　And heard a Voice call me; since then
I walk down the valley of silence,
　That lies far beyond mortal ken.

Do you ask what I find in the valley?
　'Tis my trysting-place with the Divine;
Where I fall at the feet of the Holy,
　And above me a Voice says, 'Be Mine.'
And there comes from the depths of my spirit
　An echo, — 'My heart shall be Thine.'

Do you ask how I live in the valley?
　I weep, and I dream, and I pray;
But my tears are as sweet as the dewdrops
　That fall on the roses in May;
And my prayer, like a perfume from censer,
　Ascendeth to God night and day.

In the hush of the valley of silence
　I dream all the songs that I sing;
And the music floats down the dim valley
　Till each finds a word for a wing:
That to men, like the dove of the deluge,
　The message of peace they may bring.

But far on the deep there are billows
　That never shall break on the beach;

And I have heard songs in the silence
　That never shall float into speech;
And I have had dreams in the valley
　Too lofty for language to reach;

And I have had thoughts in the valley, —
　Ah, me! how my spirit was stirred, —
They wear holy veils on their faces,
　Their footsteps can scarcely be heard;
They pass through the valley like virgins,
　Too pure for the touch of a word.

Do you ask me the place of the valley,
　Ye hearts that are harassed by care?
It lieth afar between mountains;
　And God and His angels are there.
And one is the dark Mount of Sorrow,
　And one the bright Mountain of Prayer."

Now let us study the character of this flight that is promised to the reverent, waiting soul whose trust is in God. "With wings as eagles" is the promise. Well, we know something about that. If they are like eagles' wings we know they must be wings of eager purpose. This is not the kind of wings the Psalmist was praying for when, all worn out and disheartened, he prayed, "Oh, that I had wings like a dove! for then I would fly away, and be at rest." He wanted wings with which to dodge duty; wings to escape life's work. But the wings that are promised to the waiting soul are of a very different character — they are wings of purpose.

One of the greatest causes of failure among people who set out to make the Christian flight is that they are dominated by no great, worthy purpose. All their plans are little and petty. And a man with only insignificant purposes and motives cannot help being a bore to save his life. On the other hand, a great purpose will ennoble and dignify the smallest means, and make wings out of unexpected material. An English preacher was once talking to his congregation about the heathen, and how great was their need of the Gospel. In the congregation was one little boy who became greatly interested. He went home and told his mother that he must give something to help buy Bibles for the heathen. But he and his mother were very poor, and at first he was quite puzzled to know how to raise the money. Finally he hit upon a plan. The people of England use rubbing-stones, or door-stones as they are called, for polishing their hearths and scouring their wooden floors. These stones are bits of marble or freestone begged from the stone-cutters or marble-workers; and it is quite common to see a donkey with a pair of panniers or baskets across its back, loaded with door-stones, which its boy-driver is selling. Now, this little boy whose missionary enthusiasm had been aroused had a donkey named Neddy. He thought it would be nice to have Neddy help in the good work. So he loaded him with stones, and went around calling as loud as he could cry, " Door-stones, door-stones! Do you want any door-stones?" And before long he had raised three pounds, or about fifteen dollars. So, one day, the minister heard a knock at his door, and, opening it, there stood the little boy, holding out a package, saying. —

" Please, sir, send this to the heathen."

" But, my little friend. I must have a name to acknowledge it to."

The little boy hesitated, as if he did not understand.

" You must tell me your name," repeated the minister; "that we may know who gave the money."

"Oh, well, then, sir, please put it down to Neddy and me. That will do, won't it, sir?"

So even a donkey's long ears may be changed into wings, if there be a sufficiently noble purpose at heart.

Nothing can withstand a great purpose.

A writer in an electrical journal proposed to measure thought by means of the heat developed within the brain, acting upon the thermopile. The proposition was received in some quarters with considerable scepticism: but, like many other seemingly impossible things, it has been accomplished. Not long ago a celebrated electrician stated that he could "think a hole through an inch board;" and by connecting an inch drill so that it could be actuated by the electric current produced by the concentration of his thought, he actually did it. If a man by the aid of an electric current, harnessed by his own hands, can think a hole through a solid timber, what can he not do when his purpose is supported and sustained by the power of the Holy Spirit?

Again, the wings of the eagle are wings of aspiring faith and exultant hope. He who waits upon the Lord does not find himself becalmed on waveless seas, but mounts up where heavenly trade-winds blow.

Dr. A. J. Lyman tells how he was once travelling on a steamer on Lake Superior, when he saw a wonderful sight. There was no wind on the water; it lay bright and wide without a ripple. Glancing up at the top of the tall smoke-stack he expected to see the issuing volume of smoke drifting far astern through the moveless air; but, to his great astonishment, he saw the great black coil of smoke cut off flat at the top of the smoke-stack, evidently by a powerful wind, but carried toward the bows in the very direction they were going, and streaming away through the heavens ahead of the steamer for miles. He turned to the captain, near whom he was standing, and said, "Captain, am I dreaming? Look there!" He looked, and said, "No, you are not dreaming. Perhaps half a dozen times in my thirty years on these lakes I have seen that occurrence. Fifty feet above our heads half a gale of wind is blowing, and blowing in the same direction we are going, and twice as fast, though to look at the water you would say there was not a breath. That wind is from the upper currents of the atmosphere. We are going twelve knots, and that wind is going thirty."

That which happens so rarely to a lake steamer is the thing which may be well known to him who is strong in the faith. The soul that waits upon the Lord, and mounts up with wings as eagles, enters into the domain of the heavenly trade-winds, where all things work together for good to them that love God.

The more we come to know of the grandeur of the universe, the loftier will be our flights of faith and hope.

Not long ago Sir Robert Ball, the astronomer, said in a lecture, that a telegraphic message would go seven times around the earth in a second; and if a telegraphic message could be sent to the moon, it would reach its destination in a little more than a second. It would take something like eight minutes to arrive at the sun; but to reach the nearest stars, travelling at the tremendous pace of one hundred and eighty thousand miles a second, it would take three long years to accomplish the journey; and there are stars so remote that if the news of the victory of Wellington at Waterloo had been flashed to them in 1815 on the celestial telegraph system, it would not have reached them yet. And back of them are stars yet so much farther remote, that if, when William the Conqueror landed in England, eight hundred and twenty-eight years ago, the news of his conquest had been despatched to them, the signals flying over the wire at a pace which would carry them seven times around the earth in a second of time, that news would not yet have reached them; and back of them, in the great depths of space, there are stars so far away that if the glad tidings of the angels' songs to the shepherds in Bethlehem, nearly nineteen centuries ago, had been telegraphed through the universe at the pace of a hundred and eighty thousand miles a second, the music of redemption's song would still be on the wing.

How our hearts bound within us as we come to realize that He who holds all these worlds in His hands is our Father and our Friend! Well does the Psalmist say, " Day unto day uttereth speech, and night unto night showeth knowledge."

A very interesting little story has been going the rounds of the press recently, how for a number of years a pair of storks built their nest annually in the park of an old castle in Berlin. Finally, one of the servants placed a ring marked with the date and name of the place on the male bird, in order to be certain that the same bird returned each year. This spring the stork came back to its customary place, the bearer of two rings. The second one bore the inscription, " India sends greetings to Germany." Well, that is very interesting; but what is that to the fact that heaven sends its greeting to earth with every morning sunbeam, and over the telegraph wire of faith to every prayerful soul?

The soul that enters into these high fellowships and soars out in these wide realms is able to sing with the poet, —

> " Never the ocean breathed in sleep
> A sigh however lone,
> But somewhere broke in music deep
> Upon some waiting shore;

And never a throb of heat and light
Of the sun's great heart is lost;
Through cycles of chaos beating on,
In trackless spaces crossed,
Bound for ages of icy night
In the keep of the dungeon mine,
From its prison of cold and darkness fast,
The hoarded force shall burst and shine
With the sun's own fire at last.

Never a throb of love and light
From the heart of God e'er came, —
Though the night of wrong be cruel and long, —
But shall kindle in deathless flame;
And the thought He has set to music,
Though the tempest of hate be strong,
Some time, through the strife on the shores of life,
Shall echo in living song!"

John never said anything truer than when he declared, "This is the victory that overcometh the world, even our faith." For that is the only real conquest we get over the world. A man may be able to make steam and electricity do his bidding, and yet be himself their slave, and only have added to the burdens which press down his weary shoulders. As one well says, "Steam and electricity are our masters, not we theirs. We are like hands in some great factory — the faster the wheels revolve, the more unremitting and exhausting is our work to keep up with them." When the seventy disciples came back to Christ, and told Him of their success, and were especially jubilant because the devils were subject to them, Jesus replied that they should rejoice not that the devils were subject to them, but rather rejoice because their names were written in heaven. Some one writing about Enoch the other day, commented on the fact that one day Enoch was missing; for God had taken him away, we know not how. And then, speculating about it, said, "It may have been by means of a golden chariot drawn by snow-white, winged horses, a whirlwind, a blaze of light and glory; or, possibly, angelic creatures robed in white, with far-reaching wings, gently lifted him above the earth and its cares, and conveyed him softly to the Father's bosom. But, as I read, I said to myself, "While you are at it, brother, why not suppose that he walked with God until his own wings of faith were strong enough to bear his weight, and carried him home to heaven?"

Again, they that wait upon the Lord mount

up on wings of triumphant love. The editor of the *Ram's Horn* says, "God employs no hired help." Love is the great omnipotent. In the old story, Una leads the lion about with a silken leash. Do you remember the demoniac of Gadara? All the physical force of that pork-producing community could do nothing with him; but he was like a lamb at the feet of the gentle Christ. A writer in the *Outlook*, not long ago, tells a story which occurred in a woman's club, organized in a poor tenement-house district in New York city. The purpose of this club, like that of clubs organized in the up-town districts, is social intercourse and entertainment. And each week the club invites before it some musicians, sometimes very famous people, who seem to enjoy their opportunity quite as much as the hearers enjoy theirs. One week, among the musical guests of the club, was a tenor with a charming, sympathetic voice. His singing had aroused the enthusiasm of his hearers to a white heat. He was so touched at their appreciation that, noticing that many of them were German women, he sat down at the organ, touched a few chords, and sang in German a little ballad, "I love her so." One of the members of the club, an elderly woman, seemed to be deeply moved by the song, so much so that her eyes filled with tears. When the song was finished, she leaned toward her nearest neighbor, an intimate friend, and said something in German. Her hearer burst out laughing, and then called out to the president of the club, "She says that is the song her husband always sings to her when she gets mad at him." Then the woman whose confidence had been revealed said, "It is really true. Ven I gets mad to Charlie, and vill not get glad mit him, he always sits him down and sings me dat song." Wise husband! He had caught the secret of omnipotence. Jesus in John's Gospel says, "Henceforth I call you not servants . . . but . . . friends," and this pleading love it is that gives Him such marvellous power.

Such soaring lives cannot fail of noble achievement — achievement which shall not only do honor to God and give happiness and glory to themselves, but which cannot fail to give helpfulness to others. Many of you have just been studying in the Sunday-school lessons the story of Joseph. Do you remember the words, "The Lord blessed the Egyptian's house for Joseph's sake"? And there are multitudes of beautiful illustrations not only in the Bible but in our common lives that prove the great Christian law that God often blesses one man for the sake of another. Do you remember that fearful storm on the Mediterranean Sea, when captain and sailor and soldier were alike discouraged and ready to give up in despair? But Paul stood in their midst with chained limbs, yet with a dauntless winged spirit that no chains could limit or restrain, and said, with cheerful face, "There stood by me this night the angel of God, whose I am, and whom I serve, saying, Fear not, Paul; . . . lo, God hath given thee all them that sail with thee."

So I covet for every one of us a lofty spirit, a winged soul — not for ourselves alone, but for all these brothers and sisters about us whose numbed and broken wings appeal to our sympathy and love.

XV

THE PILGRIMAGE OF FAITH

"Strangers and pilgrims on the earth."—HEB. xi. 13.

WHETHER we will or not we are all travellers. "In we are, and on we must." We cannot stand still if we would; and if we have caught anything of the true zest of life, we would not if we could. Childhood, youth, manhood, age, like the changing hours of the day and the procession of the seasons, swing us ever onward. Whether we go with all sails flying, like some queenly ship, exulting in our power, or as a helpless, broken fragment, drifting with the tide, we are ever floated onward.

To the real pilgrim this fact of necessary and inevitable progress is full of inspiration. To the mere time-killer life may be only a dull routine; but to the man who is consciously going somewhere, and going there on purpose, who has the pilgrim's spirit and courage, life is intensely real. To such an one, every day is a fresh study from the hand of God. The past to him is only a background for the romantic and interesting present.

This attitude of the pilgrim toward human life is the necessary attitude in order to high and courageous action. No man can do his greatest work without the courage and freedom which comes from this largeness of view. One may use any sort of a tent during the summer days in the mountains, or be satisfied with the rudest conveniences in a wayside camp. So to the real pilgrim the end is the chief thing, the style of travel is insignificant. If one have a sublime purpose, like the Pilgrims who came over in the Mayflower, the size of the boat or the propelling power are of small consequence. Grandeur of purpose and intensity of enthusiasm like theirs is a far more powerful motor than steam or electricity. Opposition, discouraging circumstances, sickness, pain — none of these things can move from his course or seriously hinder him who has the real spirit of the pilgrim.

Not long ago that greatest citizen of the civilized world. Mr. Gladstone, called on his physician. who is also an oculist, that he might have his eyes examined. The physician told Mr. Gladstone that a cataract had impaired the sight of one eye, and that another cataract was forming on the other. The great man reflected a moment. and said. "I wish you to remove the cataract at once." The physician replied that it was not far enough advanced for an operation. "You do not understand me," answered Mr. Gladstone. "It is the old cataract I wish removed. If that is out of the way, I shall still have one good eye when the new cataract impairs the sight of the other." As the physician still hesitated, Mr. Gladstone continued, "You still seem not to understand me. I want you to perform the operation here and now. while I am sitting in this chair." "But it might not be successful." said the doctor. "That is a risk I accept." was the instant reply. One cannot fail to see in this incident the heroic spirit of the pilgrim which has given Mr. Gladstone such victorious strides across the course of three generations.

Many young men and women who start out well in life, and in their early Christian experience give great promise of high spiritual development, are later a disappointment both to themselves and their friends from the fact that they lose the spirit of the pilgrim and settle down to be mere ranchers and herders, easily contented with the ephemeral pleasures of the present. To be content with small achievements means perpetual poverty. That noble discontent which drove the Israelites out of Egypt, drove the Pilgrim Fathers from England to Holland, and from Holland to Plymouth Rock, is similar to the spiritual discontent which drives a man out from the domain of vulgar thoughts, makes him revolt against ignoble servitudes, and sends him forth upon an upward pilgrimage, ever aspiring and striving after better things.

The possibility of high and glorious life is within the reach of every one of us. "The fault, dear Brutus," said Cassius, "is not in our stars, but in ourselves, that we are underlings." And Paul says, "When I was a child, I spake as a child, I felt as a child, I thought as a child: now that I am become a man, I have put away childish things." Would to God that that might be truthfully said of every one of us! But how many people throng the churches who, after twenty years of experience, still cling with childish hands to their bibs and nursing-bottles! A strong Christian life cannot be produced without willingness to endure trial; without the exercise which comes from hardship and exertion; without the determination to risk and dare and do for the right; without the inspiration which comes from the consciousness of self-denial in fellowship with Jesus Christ. Church membership is not intended to be a rocking-chair, where a man, attended by his pastor and class-leader, shall be soothed and quieted and rocked to and fro, but making no advancement and going nowhere. A rich Christian experience cannot be obtained except as it comes to the pilgrim who is making daily advancement. No man can acquire the experience of a European tour unless he makes it. The richest enjoyment of it consists of those things that cannot be even planned beforehand; in those unexpected personal happenings which unfold to him day by day and hour by hour. So God does not have spiritual graces stored up which He distributes to us through some set system of His own. He only can bestow these graces of the Spirit upon us as in the actual contacts of life we need them. Hunger and food are the natural complements of each other, and belong together. It is useless to try to feed a man who has no appetite, no zest, no relish for food; and even the all-wise God has not discovered how to bestow the graces of the Spirit except in answer to spiritual hunger.

Nothing is so pitiable, so hopeless, as spiritual apathy — a soul that has ceased to be dissatisfied with its own sluggish and useless life. Annie Breckett well says, "Go on and make errors, and fall and get up again. Only go on. You are made to fall over and over again, or you would never gain strength. The harder time you have, the gladder you ought to be, for you are getting exercise and experience; and then God would never spend so much trouble in training you if you were not worth the effort.

You must really be of considerable value." And Lowell sings, —

> "But two ways are offered to our will, —
>   Toil, with rare triumph; ease, with safe disgrace,
>   Nor deem that acts heroic wait on chance.
>   The man's whole life preludes the single deed
>   That shall decide if his inheritance
>   Be with the sifted few of matchless breed,
>   Or with the unmotived herd that only sleep and feed."

We have a modern invention called the time-lock — a combination of clockwork with the lock of a vault or safe, which renders it impossible for any key to open the door until a certain hour. When the door is locked and the clock is set for a definite time, until that hour comes the banker or merchant is as helpless as any burglar or thief; the safe cannot be opened or its contents obtained. There is something like that in God's spiritual economy in relation to the pilgrims of the faith. Good things are stored up for us all along the way of life, but on every storehouse of blessing there is the time-lock of God's providential care. No man can force the door on to-morrow's mercies and obtain them for to-day's use. There ought to be great comfort in this for us; and it ought to reveal to us the uselessness of worry and anxiety which seem to hover like clouds about the horizon of to-morrow. When to-morrow's difficulties are really present, the time-lock on God's new mercies shall open the door of His love and provision for us. We do not have to pass through the floods until they come. Yet some people do feel the chill of imaginary floods more than the real ones. A clever and charming old lady once said to a group of girl admirers gathered for a talk. " My dears, you wonder that nothing ever seems to annoy me. Some people, you know, have their trouble three times (I used to have): first in anticipation, next in experiencing the reality, and lastly in living it all over again. But I have made up my mind that to have trouble once is enough. Thus I escape two-thirds the worry that I would otherwise have." The pilgrim need not worry about the waters to which he has not yet come. When you do come there the promise is, " When thou passest through the waters, I will be with thee." Daniel's three friends did not find the fire slackening when they were cast into the furnace. So fierce was it that the men who cast them in were destroyed, and yet God's time-lock did not fail — for the form of the fourth, like unto the Son of man, met them at the furnace door; and not even the smell of fire was on their garments. And so the promise is for you. "When thou walkest through the fire, thou shalt not be burned."

One of the greatest of mistakes is to give ourselves anxiety because we cannot get a panoramic view of what the future holds for us. It is the very essence of our pilgrimage that we walk by faith and not by sight. This world is a twilight land at best. We see through a glass darkly. And yet ever and anon God does give us glimpses sufficient for our encouragement and inspiration. As Lucy Larcom sings, —

> " Life comes to us only by glimpses;
>   We see it not yet as a whole,
> For the vapor, the cloud, and the shadow
>   That over it surging roll;
> For the dimness of mortal vision,
>   That mingles the false with the true;
> Yet its innermost, fathomless meaning
>   Is never quite hidden from view.

Life shows us its grandeur by glimpses;
    For what is this wondrous To-day
But a rift in the mist-muffled vastness
    Of surrounding eternity?
One law for this hour and far futures;
    One light on the distant and near,
The bliss of the boundless hereafter
    Pulses into the brief moments here.

The secret of life, — it is giving,
    To minister and to serve;
Love's law binds the man to the angel,
    And ruin befalls if we swerve.
There are breadths of celestial horizons
    Overhanging the commonest way;
The clod and the star share the glory,
    And to breathe is an ecstasy.

Life dawns on us, wakes us, by glimpses;
    In heaven there is opened a door,—
That flash lit up vistas eternal;
    The dead are the living once more!
To illumine the scroll of creation,
    One swift, sudden vision sufficed:
Every riddle of life worth the reading
    Has found its interpreter — Christ!

All pilgrims find the friendships and fellowships which they form on their pilgrimage to be the chief sources of their joy and strength. The rich brotherhood which comes to those who share hardships, who bear common burdens, who risk mutual dangers, can only be appreciated by those who have experienced them. The fellowships which come to the pilgrims of the faith are very sweet and precious. He who has the Spirit of Jesus Christ, who has come to walk in harmony with Him, has a vision of the brotherhood of humanity which can be acquired on no other plane. The true pilgrim of the faith recognizes all fellow-travellers as his brothers. In his address on Democracy, James Russell Lowell relates the beautiful and profound parable of the Persian poet Jelâl-ed-Deen, who tells us, "One knocked at the Beloved's door, and a voice from within asked, 'Who is there?' and he answered, 'It is I.' Then the voice said, 'This house will not hold thee and me.' And the door was not opened. Then went the lover into the desert and fasted and prayed in solitude; and after a year he returned and knocked again at the door, and again the voice asked, 'Who is there?' and he said, 'It is thyself.' And the door was opened to him."

Life's supreme object is to realize love for man; to translate into human action the divine spirit revealed in the words, God so loved the world that He gave His Son. If the pilgrimage of life is doing that for you, then it is really bringing you onward toward heaven. Spurgeon said of an old Puritan, that heaven was in him before he was in heaven. And an old Scotchman, who was asked whether he ever expected to get to heaven, replied, "Why, man, I live there!"

The spirit of the pilgrim is the spirit of promptitude. One essential characteristic of success must be the doing of everything in its place and time. As we pass this way but once, we cannot afford to delay or to put off to-day's duty until to-morrow. Josephine Pollard tells of an inn among the mountains of Switzerland where tourists are accustomed to stop and refresh themselves before making a grand ascent. In the waiting-room of this hotel was a placard suspended in plain sight, containing in large type these three words, "Do it now." When the innkeeper was asked the meaning of this, he explained that he was continually bothered by tourists asking him when they should make this or that preparation for their mountain tours, and so he had had the placard put up that it might save him the trouble of answering so many questions. That innkeeper was a philosopher; for, no doubt, many a tourist has had occasion to thank him for that silent but impressive warning against the danger of procrastination. Do we not need the same warning? Hanging at the gateway of the duties of every day, of every hour, should be the impressive, imperative warning, Do it now. The word of apology you owe to your wife, or husband, or friend, or servant, or employer; the message of sympathy you are moved to speak or write to a broken heart; the help which your hand itches to give to an impoverished brother — all these and many other opportunities and privileges of life's pilgrimage must be seized upon at once, or they are lost.

To him who enters upon life daily as a pilgrimage, and who walks among his fellows in the spirit of the democracy of Jesus Christ, common life abounds in romantic interest. Everything is full of interest to the sympathetic and sensitive soul. Mr. Gladwyn sings a little song that ought to be especially comforting and refreshing to those who, like myself, spent their childish days among the fields and pastures of the country. He says, —

"All along the wayside is everybody's garden!
There the wild rose blossoms through the summer days;
Bounded by field fences, and ever stretching onward,
It is God's own garden. For it give Him praise.
    'Tis gay with golden-rod;
    There blooming grasses nod,
And sun-flowers small and yellow turn ever to the sun;
    Quaint darkey heads are there,
    And daisies wild and fair.
In everybody's garden each flower's the loveliest one!

All along the wayside is everybody's garden!
Come out and gather posies; the very air is sweet.
Come out with hearts of gladness, ye big and little children,
Into our Father's garden, made for our strolling feet.
    The flitting butterfly,
    The fragrant winds that sigh,
The tiny clouds that hover above us in the blue,
    The bird's song high and clear,
    Make heaven draw more near.
In everybody's garden the world once more is new!"

And in spite of all sorrow and wrong and sin, our every-day life is everybody's garden to him whose heart is sensitive enough to reproduce the joy which the good God bestows upon us.

No greater mistake can be made than to imagine that the people with whom we are thrown are of such a commonplace kind that the deep pathos and romance of life is not revealed in them. Notice what commonplace people Jesus had to deal with — blind Bartimæus, begging beside the road; the woman with the waterpot by the well in Samaria, a vulgar sort of woman who had had five husbands and got on with none of them; Simon's mother-in-law, who had a fever; some fishermen who had had bad luck, and so on. And yet in every one of these, and multitudes of others like them, was to Jesus Christ a gold-mine of entertainment and interest and opportunity for rich spiritual development. Our neighbor, the Rev. John W. Chadwick, creates a beautiful aphorism when he says, "There is a better thing than realizing the ideal; it is to idealize the real." And nothing will do that so well as to approach all life in a spirit of brotherly sympathy and fellowship.

Old age can have no terror to the genuine pilgrim of the faith. I think it is Emerson who in his last years sang, —

> "As the bird trims her to the gale,
>   I trim myself to the storm of time.
> I man the rudder, reef the sail,
>   Obey the voice at eve obeyed at prime,
> Lowly faithful, banish fear,
>   Right onward drive unharmed;
> The port, well worth the cruise, is near,
>   And every wave is charmed."

There is no sorrow in accumulated years to such a soul. The historian tells us that when Columbus was at last drawing near to the shores of America, the waves and the sky brought him many indications that he was approaching the land. Birds hovered above his vessel, and at last alighted on the masts and seemed to sing songs of the shore. Branches of trees with ripened berries on them were caught up from the waves by the wondering and happy sailors and eaten with delight. Old age to the Christian pilgrim is like that. As he nears the heavenly shores rich fruitage from the tree of life floats out to him on the welcoming tide. Angels of immortal hope hover over him and sing strains of heavenly music in his enraptured ears.

To the pilgrim of the faith death is not a

stopping-place, a terminus, but only a transfer station. "A crown of life" is the promise. Hear the message given to John: Endure thou unto death, and thou shalt receive a crown of life. And James says, "Blessed is the man that endureth temptation : for when he hath been approved, he shall receive the crown of life, which the Lord promised to them that love him." What a noble reward is this! It is not anything that could appeal to the sluggish or selfish soul ; but the reward of a good life here is to be a complete and enlarged life hereafter. We are to be clothed upon with immortality. " For we know that if the earthly house of our tabernacle be dissolved, we have a building from God, a house not made with hands, eternal, in the heavens." We leave a pilgrim's tent to go to a heavenly mansion. "Life and thought," says the poet, of the translated pilgrim. —

> " have gone away, side by side,
> Leaving doors and windows wide;
> Careless tenants they!"

And they can well afford to be careless, for glorious provision has been made for them beyond.

We do not know a great deal about the architecture of the homes to which we are going, but there are some things we know we will not need. They will need no storm windows to keep out the storms in winter, no bolts and bars against burglars, no screens against mosquitoes in the summer, and no cedar closets to hide precious raiment from the moths. Ah, who can imagine an architecture grand enough for a free soul that has passed forever beyond the reach of fear or care or sorrow? What broad windows, what lofty domes, what musical arches, what splendor of beauty, shall there greet us we do not know. Eye hath not seen, nor ear heard, the glories which God has reserved for His children.

And what treasures await us at the end of our pilgrimage! Sometimes the traveller in foreign lands gathers many a rare painting, and beautiful pieces of sculpture and precious curios, and ships them across the sea, that, after a while, when his journeys are over, he may come back and enjoy them all at home. So the true pilgrim of the faith is constantly sending treasures across to the heavenly land. Every cup of cold water given in the name of the disciple, every deed of self-denying love, is stored in yonder heavenly mansion. And how many priceless treasures in the loved ones whom God has given us along life's pilgrimage have taken passage thitherward and await our coming. How splendid the home-coming will be when we strike camp for the last time and make our triumphant entry into the city of God!

> "Foursquare it lies, with walls of gleaming pearl,
>   And gates that are not shut at all by day:
> There evermore their wings the storm-winds furl,
>   And night falls not upon the shining way
> Up which, by twos and threes, and in great throngs,
>   The happy people tread, whose mortal road
> Led straight to that fair home of endless songs,
>   The city, beautiful and vast, of God.
>
> Eye hath not seen, ear hath not heard, the joy,
>   The light, the bloom of that sweet dwelling-place;
> Where praise is aye the rapturous employ
>   Of those who there behold God's loving face.
> Here, fretted by so many a tedious care,
>   And bowed by burdens on the weary road,
> We cannot dream of all the glory there,
>   In that bright city, beautiful, of God.
>
> There some have waited for our coming long,
>   Blown thither on the mystic tide of death;

They catch some fragments of our broken song,
　The while the eternal years are as a breath.
There we shall go one gladsome day of days,
　And drop forever every cumbering load,
And we shall view, undimmed by earth's low haze,
　The city, beautiful and vast, of God.

In that great city we shall see the King,
　And tell Him how He took us by the hand,
And let us, in our weakness, drag and cling
　As children when they do not understand,
Yet with the mother walk as night comes on,
　And wish that home was on some shorter road.
Oh, with what pleasure we shall look upon
　Our Saviour in the city of our God!"

XVI

THE WELL-DIGGERS IN THE VALLEY OF BACA

"Who passing through the valley of Baca make it a well."
— PSALMS lxxxiv. 6.

BISHOP WILLIAM TAYLOR, the "Grand Old Man" of modern missions, is called the "well-digger" by the native tribes in many parts of Africa, because of his habit of digging wells with his own hands wherever he goes, securing that way not only his own comfort, but giving blessing to others who come to the wayside wells and slake their thirst long after the busy leader of the Lord's frontier hosts has passed on to bless other lands.

Now, our text assures us that the good bishop is only a type of what occurs in higher and more spiritual ways wherever God's pilgrims travel. Though they pass through the valley of Baca, or the land where only "tear shrubs" grow, they by their presence and labor produce wells of comfort in the midst of desolation. There could not be a more striking illustration of the blessing of true souls who live in communion with God than the figure used here.

It is hard for us to appreciate it in well-watered New England, even when we are assured that our Boston water supply is just now threatened by the long season of dry weather; but in a land where rains seldom fall a well is a matter about which wars might easily arise between neighboring nations.

We are told that some years since the Czar of Russia had determined upon the extension of his empire eastward from the Caspian. "Sire, it is impossible," said his engineers. "Between the Salt Sea and Bokhara lies a desert of death. It is white with the bones of dromedaries. Man may not cross it and live." "Fill it with water," said the Czar. And with the derrick and the drill the underlying rock was pierced. Forthwith rose the living streams; and now across the wilderness of dust is threaded upon a necklace of steel the emerald oases, beautiful with the almond and oleander.

It was hardly to be wondered at that the Hebrew multitudes thought themselves scarcely saved when they emerged from the sea only to plunge into the great and terrible wilderness of Arabia, "where no water is." But the word of Jehovah made the rocks to give forth fountains; and wherever the cloudy pillar stopped the wilderness became a well.

Out on the high table-lands, between the Missouri and the Rocky Mountains, a station on one of the Pacific railways is named Wells, because in the midst of the dry plain the railroad company has bored down into the heart of the earth, and tapped hidden streams that flow from the mountain reservoirs hundreds of miles away.

The great theme we are to study, then, is this, that there is no valley of hardship or trial so severe but that by faith and earnest exertion we may make it fertile; that if we go deep enough into the sands of trouble, and find God's purpose for us, we shall find wells of living water to refresh our thirsty souls.

Such wells may be found by those who feel themselves narrowed and pinched in their business relations by the present pressure of hard times. Two men were coming out of church after listening to a sermon on God's interest in the least affairs of daily life. Both were Christians, and naturally fell to speaking about the thought of the morning. "It is difficult for me to believe," said one, "that the great God really cares anything about the details of my business." "Oh," responded the other, "but that's just the comfort I find in my religion." Surely no one, be his cares few or many, has grasped the real blessing of religion until he realizes that the things which are of moment to him are of equal concern to the Father of us all. Many business men in these trying days are finding out for the first time what God's love and care really mean. A St. Louis merchant in a private letter says, "Sometimes of late it has seemed to me that the only thing left was a consciousness of duty done to the best of my ability and a reliance upon the promises."

Much of business life is permeated with such a spirit of selfishness and greed, that hard times would be a blessing in disguise if it brought to business men more of a feeling of sympathy and brotherhood in their trouble. A suggestive scene occurred in the New York Stock Exchange the other day, as reported by the New York *Tribune.* In the midst of the babel of voices came the rapping of the chairman's gavel, the prelude to the announcement of a failure. "The bears," we read, "rushed toward the rostrum with a shout of exultation to hear what the chairman had to say, and to learn the name of the firm that was in trouble." Think of it! "a shout of exultation" because a firm had failed. Surely the actors in such a stock market are well named "bulls" and "bears." As one reads of such an occurrence, one can almost see the sharp horns piercing the screaming victim, or the fierce claws as they tear the lacerated flesh. A valley of Baca in the business world would be a cause for national thanksgiving, if there might come out of it some redemption from scenes like that.

But any business man who by his perplexities is led to a clearer view of the fatherhood of God and a tenderer vision of the brotherhood of man, will make a well of peace for himself and others.

I read the other day the story of a gardener. The grapes in his vineyard were just beginning to ripen. He wanted to find a few bunches for a friend who was visiting him. They went out together. "See here," the friend said, "this bunch hangs in the sunshine; it must be riper than those which are in the shade." He plucked it, put a grape in his mouth, made a wry face, and when the gardener asked what was the matter, replied, "Those grapes were well colored; they looked as if they were ripe; but I find on tasting them that they are hard and sour. We won't get any fruit here that is fit to eat to-day." "Wait a moment," said the gardener. And going to a vine that looked as if it had nothing on it except leaves, he lifted a drooping branch, and picked from it a bunch that had grown in the shade. It had not the sun-tint upon its berries which attracted his friend in the bunch he had gathered, but a delicate yellowish color which told of mellowness and sweetness. The gardener handed it to him. He tasted it and said, "Why, that is splendid! How did it ripen so, away down there under the leaves?" "Ah," said the gardener, "I cannot explain the how and why, but I have learned by long experience in vineyards and orchards that if you want to find the earliest, the juiciest, and the sweetest fruit, you must look for it under the leaves." It is not the direct rays of the sun, but those rays softened and mellowed by passing through the foliage that gives us the best grapes and peaches. The man who picked all the leaves from his trees in order to facilitate the ripening of his fruit, found it scorched and shrivelled by the sunshine. The Lord's way is to blend the sunshine and shade. Too much of either is disastrous. In a well-cultivated vineyard or orchard He will see to it that a due proportion is preserved. And so He will in our lives if we trust in Him and obey Him and try to serve Him. Did you ever ponder that statement of the bride in Canticles ii. 3, "I sat down under his shadow with great delight, and his fruit was sweet to my taste"? She knew where to find the ripest apples. She did not stand out in the sunshine, but went under the tree. There in the shade she enjoyed the fruit that was sweetened through the leaves. I have read of an aged pauper who was found at the county infirmary with a Bible in his lap, reading it slowly through his spectacles, keeping the place with one of his fingers, which moved under the lines. When asked, "What are you doing, old man?" he looked up with the smile of an angel on his wrinkled face, and said, "Oh, sir, I am sitting under His shadow with great delight, and His fruit is sweet to my taste." He never appreciated the preciousness of the promises in his days of health and prosperity as he did when overshadowed by weakness, poverty, and pain. The Psalmist says, "He that dwelleth in the secret place of the most High shall abide under the shadow of the Almighty." He shall be protected from the sunshine, because God loves him and wants to ripen his character.

It is in the midst of toil's severe testing that the sweetest flowers of our civilization bloom. The great pictures of our own time prove this. The one the whole world has been struggling after, "The Angelus," is so small a canvas one might carry it in a valise, and yet the heart of mankind has taken it up and glorified it. Why? Because it speaks to us of the rich veins of gold which lie in common mortals, the kind of people who wear blue denims and calico, and dig potatoes in common fields. If the two worshipful figures in "The Angelus" had represented some statesman like Gladstone and some poetess like Mrs. Browning, it would have been the curiosity of the hour and nothing more; but now it stands for humanity.

In the most toilworn life of the weariest traveller through the valley of Baca there are wells of reverence, of worship, of communion with God.

You may see this great truth illustrated everywhere. Unusual interest was excited recently in New York city by the passing from North River *via* Washington Square, and, with a rest under the Washington Arch, to Broadway, and down that thoroughfare to the Pennsylvania railroad ferry, of the "Columbian Liberty Bell" on its way to the World's Fair. The bell, weighing thirteen thousand pounds, was not easy to move. It took twenty-five men two hours to load it upon the trucks, and six stalwart horses to draw it. Six grenadier policemen guarded the truck. Mr. Meneely, the founder of the bell, and some of his family, followed in a carriage; and interested crowds thronged the way as the bell, draped in the national flag, held its slow course to the landing, to be taken by rail through Philadelphia, Baltimore, Washington, Pittsburg, etc., to Chicago. The bell, made up of intrinsically precious, and sentimentally more precious. materials from our own and other lands, will bear a notable part in coming events here and abroad. Its voice is already bespoken for celebrating many weighty historical events closely bearing on the progress of human freedom. Why did it wake this enthusiasm as it passed along the streets of the great metropolis? Because it spoke to their hearts a story of sacrifice, of volunteers who, on the march, in camp, on battle-field, in hospitals, and in a hundred ways, suffered and endured and died that out of their " valley of Baca " these bells might forever peal the music of liberty.

Sickness, or personal affliction, is a valley of

Baca which may be, and often is, fertile because of the wells dug by trusting hands.

Fanny Crosby, the blind poetess, who has written so many inspiring hymns, addressed the late Northfield (Mass.) meeting as follows: —

"Dear friends, I am here once more in the beautiful village of Northfield, which sleeps so tranquilly among the mountains. God's peace hovers over this place and in this sacred house. Year by year, as they go by, seems to bind me more closely to this place. It is my home, and the ties of friendship grow stronger and stronger. I thought to-day how grand it will be when we meet in that land where we need never part! Mr. and Mrs. Baker and I do not regret that we cannot see. We have our mind, our intellect. We can picture every face : and, what is more, we have our faith centred in the 'Rock of Ages.' Do we regret it? No. When we enter the pearly gates God's face will be the first on which we gaze. Oh, how small the sorrow of this world as compared with the joy of that meeting!"

She then closed with the following original poem : —

'Some day my earthly house will fall,
 I cannot tell how soon 'twill be;
But this I know, — my All in All
 Has now in heaven a place for me,
And I shall see Him face to face,
And tell the story, — saved by grace.

Some day the silver cord will break,
 And I no more as now shall sing;
But, oh, the joy when I shall wake
 Within the palace of the King!
And I shall see Him face to face,
And tell the story, — saved by grace.

Some day, when fades the golden sun
 Beneath the hazy-tinted west,
My blessed Lord shall say, 'Well done,'
 And I shall enter into rest;
And I shall see Him face to face,
And tell the story, — saved by grace.

Some day! till then I'll watch and wait,
 My lamp all trimmed and burning bright,
That when the Saviour opes the gate
 My soul to Him may wing its flight,
And I shall see Him face to face,
And tell the story, — saved by grace."

Old age is a valley of Baca which we can make largely what we please. Two women of middle age, but in the full plenitude of health and strength, sat watching the twilight of a summer evening creep over the landscape, when one of them suddenly inquired, "What do you dread most in connection with old age?" A thoughtful pause, and then came the reply, "Not the failure of sight or hearing, not the paralysis of limbs or memory, but the loss of love. I can imagine nothing more dreadful than to be left alone in the world with no one to especially care for me." The words embody a common sentiment of dread among people who are approaching the sunset slopes of life; but it is more a matter of personal control than we are apt to think whether or no we have a loveless old age. We have seen multitudes of elderly people, some of them the sole survivors of a large family, helpless and dependent, it may be, whose presence, nevertheless, was a delight in the household. Providence may shut the door of heaven between ourselves and our kindred; but by our own volition we close our hearts and narrow our lives, and thereby prepare for loss of love in old age.

And then we must not forget that we are only pilgrims in the valley of Baca. We do not live there — we are only passing through. We dig our wells for a day and a night, and go on and leave them; but the fresh strength and courage we carry with us.

I was talking the other day with a man who superintended the putting up of a telegraph line in Persia. Much of their work was across sandy deserts, where they had to dig for their drinking-water. They had a regular well-digging department that went on ahead of the working-force, until an appropriate camping-place was found; and then they set to work and drove a well, which furnished them water for the night and was deserted the next morning. Our Christian pilgrimage is like that. We may be passing through the valley of desolation, where digging wells is hard work; but we are passing through, and it will soon be only a memory covered with the golden haze which memory casts. We shall not stay in the valley of "tear shrubs"— we are on our way home. When an overland train from the West unloads its passengers at the railroad station, there are always multitudes of eager faces there watching to welcome their weary and travel-stained friends; so there are watching at heaven's gates eager faces to greet the travellers from this world.

In a large hall in the Vatican, called the Hall of Inscriptions, there are set in the plaster of the wall on one side fifteen hundred broken marbles taken from the tombs of pagan Rome. Upon that wall rests all the shadow of death in all its natural terror. You will search in vain among all those hundreds of marbles for one single word of comfort or one ray of hope; but when you turn about to the opposite side of the hall your heart is strangely lightened, for there you find fifteen hundred inscriptions taken from the catacombs, and the beauty of Easter morning glorifies the great chamber. However rudely the epitaph is written, or however elaborately the memorial is embellished, on every side the words of rest, joy, hope, and reunion greet your glad eyes. It is impossible to describe the rebound of the heart from the depression of one side of the chamber to the exaltation of the other.

Let the glory of our Christian faith give gladness to our hearts while we are passing through our valley of Baca. We have only to be faithful to God and we shall find wells sufficient to sustain and comfort us until we stand by the River of Life.

XVII

AN ENTHUSIASM FOR HUMANITY

[FROM AN ADDRESS DELIVERED AT THE ANNUAL MEETING OF THE BROOKLYN CHURCH SOCIETY HELD IN SIMPSON M. E. CHURCH, BROOKLYN, N.Y., APRIL 26, 1894.]

AN enthusiasm for humanity itself is needed in the church more than anything else. It is easy enough for most of us to believe that humanity as represented in our own family, or in our little coterie of particular friends, is a precious thing. But this is in no sense the Christian view. To Jesus Christ all humanity was sacred and precious. Not because it was rich or learned, or lovable to the eye of sense, but because every man is a child of God. We must have that estimate of humanity.

I was riding over in northern New York a few months ago in a sleeping-car at night.

Two men from Montana, who had been making a tour in the East, and were on their way home, occupied the section behind me. They were both miners, and their talk all through the evening was about mines. Finally one of these men told the other about a certain gulch up in the Montana mountains which widened as it came down out of the foot-hills into the valley, until at its mouth it was eight miles across from one mountain bluff to the other; and he said (now, he may have lied; miners will do that sometimes) that the soil was so rich in gold across that entire eight miles that you could pull up a bunch of sage-brush anywhere, and shake the dust off from the roots into a gold pan, and get the color of gold. As I listened I said to myself, "My friend, I don't know whether you are telling the truth or not; but one thing I do know, I could go into the dirtiest, filthiest alley in Boston or New York or Brooklyn, and pick out the most ignorant and neglected specimen of childhood, some little sage-brush fragment of human life that slept last night in an ash-barrel, and if I shake him over the gold scales of heaven,

God and the angels will see that there is a vein of gold there that is worth more than the proudest business block on Broadway or Fulton Street." When the church really feels this and believes it, there will be money enough to carry on such societies as the one whose anniversary we celebrate to-night.

It is only by hand-to-hand work — one loving, self-sacrificing human brother going face to face to his brother with the message of Christ's love and God's sympathy — that we are to capture the unchurched multitudes in the cities for Christ. We must make the people feel and know that we have the same spirit toward them that Jesus Christ had and has. Coming over on the train from Boston this afternoon, I opened that really strong book, in spite of its fantastic title, " The Heavenly Twins," in the introduction to which a story is told of an old river boatman and a half-grown young lad who helped him. They were drifting along the river, when the chime from the cathedral tower rang out its sweet music on the evening air. The old boatman asked the boy if he knew the verse that usually went with the tune, and then quoted it. —

"He, watching over Israel, slumbers not, nor sleeps."

After a moment's silence the boy inquired, "Who's He?"

The old man replied, "I guess it's Christ."

"I never heard tell on Him," answered the boy.

"Never heard tell of Christ?" said the old man. "I thought every one knowed Him!"

Then the boy answered, "I don't know no one by the name of Christ; and, what's more, I am sure He don't work down our way."

Brothers, let us take the sorrowful truth home to our hearts, that there are multitudes of people in our shops and factories and streets to whom Christ is not so presented that they can believe that He still walks in fellowship with men. It is for us to reveal to them in flesh and bone the tender, brotherly, sympathetic, burden-sharing, burden-bearing Christ of old.

XVIII

TALMAGE AND HIS WORK

[AN ADDRESS DELIVERED AT THE QUARTER-CENTENNIAL CELEBRATION IN BROOKLYN TABERNACLE, MAY 10, 1894.]

OVER in the Oregon hills, where I spent my boyhood, on May afternoons like these we are now revelling in, the boys and girls on going home from the old log schoolhouse, to which many of us walked three or four miles every day, had a favorite custom of gathering wildflowers — lamb's tongues and honeysuckle, and all those quaint, old-fashioned beauties of the country hillside. And each bringing his share, some one who was skilful at it would weave a wreath, which we placed on the head of the one who was elected chief for the evening of the school group. I am very glad, Mr. Chairman, of the opportunity of bringing my little handful of wild-flowers from the Oregon hillsides, where I first came to know and admire Dr. Talmage, and add them to the garland we are weaving for the head of the most widely known chieftain of the American pulpit — indeed, I doubt not, the most universally read of all preachers now living in the world.

I am glad to do this for several reasons. First, because Dr. Talmage has, in my judgment, done more to revolutionize preaching in respect to its being made entertaining and interesting than any other man now among us. I think it is safe to say that in an overwhelming majority of the churches of the country it is no longer considered a crime for a sermon to be interesting, and that a reputation for ponderous dulness is coming to be a less winning characteristic in a preacher every year. Both the pulpit and the pew have great reason to thank Dr. Talmage for his influence in this direction.

It is equally true to say that no other minister of our time has done so much to give consecrated individuality the right of way. I believe that in no other way has humanity lost so much as in the repression of individuality. Against the tendency to cut all ministers off the same piece of cloth, make them up in the same style, and hold them to a sort of sanctified dudeism, midway between a corpse-like dignity and pious imbecility, Dr. Talmage has stood as a pulpit Gibraltar; and thousands of young ministers, encouraged by his example and inspired by his independence, have been brave enough to be themselves, and live their own life and do their own work in their own way.

Again, I am glad to be here and give my word of thanksgiving for the glorious optimism that has always shone from this pulpit. During all this twenty-five years the Tabernacle pulpit has rung out with a bright and cheering faith in a God who, having made the world, was able to take care of it and bring it at last to a successful issue. Though Dr. Talmage has preached much of the sins and the vices of the community, he has never failed to present a Christ mighty in love and power and sympathy to save the lowest and the vilest, and bring them to spiritual health and saintship. I rejoice in this; for it seems to me that above everything else the careworn, sin-burdened, despairing hearts of men need to catch the optimism of Jesus Christ, and be led with Him to see Satan, like lightning, falling from heaven, first in the horizon of their own lives, and then in the wider horizon of the human race. This is not the devil's world — it is God's; and we all ought to be able to sing with Arthur Clough, —

> "For while the tired waves, vainly breaking,
> Seem here no painful inch to gain;
> Far back, through creeks and inlets making,
> Comes, silent, flooding in, the main."

There is another thing for which I greatly honor Dr. Talmage. Notwithstanding his intense individuality, and the marvellous personal success and triumph which have come to him, he has not preached himself from this pulpit, but his sermons have glowed with reverence and loyalty to the Lord Jesus Christ. No preacher is great enough to preach safely to the people any other model save Jesus Christ. Coming down the main walks from the Capitol at Washington towards Pennsylvania Avenue, there are groups of steps that are very confusing to the average pedestrian; and a very queer story has recently been told by a Washington newspaper man concerning their construction. For years there was a man about the Capitol who made the study of steps and persons going up and down stairs a fad, and in a certain way a science. In watching crowds walking down the long approaches to the Capitol, he discovered that more people stumbled on those steps than ought to, in harmony with his records. The attention of the present Capitol architect was called to the matter, but he was incredulous about it. "Why," said he, "Frederick Olmstead, the architect, took special pains with those groups of steps, I know." However, they watched the tripping groups of steps, and discovered that the number of persons who stumbled going up, and either fell or seemed inclined to fall in descending, was really astonishing. Finally the matter was brought to the attention of Mr. Olmstead, and he went down to watch the steps himself. He was amazed to see how the people behaved when they reached those steps. He said, "I cannot account for it. I spent weeks arranging the proportion of rise to tread for them. Wooden models of them were put down for use at my own place, and I walked over them day after day, till I felt sure they were perfect." "Olmstead, isn't one of your legs a trifle shorter than the other?" inquired the step expert. Olmstead was dumbfounded when it flashed on him that, owing to the inequality in the length of his legs, he had made steps to the Capitol that were not suited for anybody except people who had the same defect in their limbs. Alas! I fear there is a good deal of preaching of that sort in the country — a good many stairways set up toward heaven that bear all the defects of the men after whose walk they have been modelled. It has been the glory of this pulpit that while no preacher in America has had more characteristic individuality, he has preached not himself, but "Jesus only."

Again, I am here to thank Dr. Talmage for showing us how a man can go on year after year doing an enormous amount of work of every sort and still keep ever fresh and new as a May morning. And yet, after all, an interest in humanity, a faith in God, an enthusiasm for good causes — these are the things that make us immortal. And nobody makes a greater blunder than to suppose that the people who carry the great burdens of the world on their heart, and throw themselves in the thick of the fight, are to be pitied or commiserated as being the burdened members of the community. On the other hand, nobody else has such a keen, appetizing, joyous life. Brooke Herford, going across Boston Common one day, met Phillips Brooks. The great bishop, towering far above him, looking down into his friend's face, saw that he was not in his usual spirits; he seemed oppressed. "What is the matter, Herford?" inquired Brooks. And Herford said, "Oh, it is hard work undertaking to make the world go straight." "That's so," said Brooks, as his cheery laugh rang out: "but then, what fun it is!" I am sure that it is this touch with all the world, this giving out of himself constantly, that keeps Dr. Talmage such a well-spring of living force. Balzac founds one of his novels on the story of the magic skin, that invested the man who wore it with a strange power to obtain whatever he desired; but every time his wish was gratified his skin shrivelled and shrank, until after a while it squeezed the life out of him. So there are multitudes of people all about us who are clutching at all the good things of God's world, and holding on to them, and never letting go, who are being smothered to death by their own prosperity. It is only the ever giving that shall be ever new.

God bless Dr. Talmage! May the future be yet more magnificent and glorious! I am sure that in the spirit of the faith which he preaches to others, he can sing with Browning, —

"Grow old along with me!
The best is yet to be,
The last of life, for which the first was made;
Our times are in His hand
Who saith, 'A whole I planned;
Youth shows but half; trust God: see all, nor be afraid!'"

XIX

SPIRITUAL AND OTHER LESSONS FROM THE PRESIDENT'S INAUGURATION.

FOR weeks past a great throng has been gathering in the city justly named for the father of his country. Every day added to the thousands journeying thither. Saturday, March 4, witnessed beside the Potomac a marvellous gathering. From all parts of the vast domain of the stars and stripes the visitors came.

Pause for a moment and think what a country it is. From the lumbering-camps of Maine, and from other lumbering-camps three thousand miles to the westward, on the shores of Puget Sound; from the cattle ranges of Texas and Colorado; from the mountains of Idaho and Tennessee; from the salmon canneries on the Columbia, and the rice-fields and sugar plantations of Mississippi; from the orange groves of

Florida by the Atlantic, and from other orange groves in California by the Pacific; from the manufactories of New England, and from the empire-like grain fields of the middle West; from the twin cities of Minnesota, and the quaint old crescent town of the Dismal Swamp of Louisiana, the visitors come to put the wand of power in the hand of their fellow-citizen. No other country on earth could send such a diversified host to its capital seat as this. They are of all nationalities. The blood of every great historic race flows in their veins, and all the languages spoken in the capitals of the world find company here.

What do they go to see? One of the grandest as well as one of the most significant spectacles of the nineteenth century — a man who, for four years, has been the ruler of more than sixty millions of people, wielding a power far more real than that exercised by the English Queen, quietly stepping aside, relinquishing army and navy and official patronage of every kind; stepping out on the plane of the simple American citizen, with only the power of his single ballot left, which he shares in common with the barber who clips his beard, or the man who blacks his boots, or the coachman who grooms his horse.

That is one part of the spectacle — the negative side of the picture. The positive side attracts most attention. The picture has been painting for months. Last autumn, from one side of the nation to the other, the people were in the midst of deep and anxious debate over a coming presidential election. The two great parties grappled in a tremendous struggle for mastery. The fateful day came. Individual sovereigns from office and shop and farm, from engine and loom and forge, registered their choice for President. Before dawn of the next morning the electric currents had carried the news to the whole civilized world that a certain citizen candidate had been chosen President of the United States. During all the months since then, however, he has been only a private citizen. He was only that up to last Saturday at twelve o'clock, and would have been promptly arrested and jailed if he had undertaken any authority of government before noon of March 4th. Yet this simple American citizen was, when the hour arrived, invested with a prouder wand of authority than is wielded by any other potentate on earth, because he has been chosen by a nation of sovereigns.

This spectacle ought to impress us with the necessity of keeping the ballot pure. No crime is more heinous than crimes against the purity of the ballot. It is only a government of the people, by the people, and for the people when a majority of the intelligent will-power of the whole country chooses our rulers and makes our laws. And how can we say that without a twinge of conscience and a blush of shame when we remember that fully one-half of the choosing power of the American people has had no voice in deciding who shall be the President of the country? This aristocracy of sex which says a man may choose who shall govern him, but a woman may not, cannot very long withstand the democratic atmosphere of our times. The keener sense of justice, the higher and truer appreciation of the worth of the individual soul which the ever-widening sway of Christianity is making prevalent, will, ere long, overflow and sweep out to sea the fossil prejudices of darker times. God speed the day when woman shall stand beside her brothers with the ballot as her guaranty of her full right of choice!

But we should fail to learn one of the great and pertinent lessons the inauguration has for us if we did not look higher yet, and remember that our fathers, in granting the right of choice to the individual American citizen, only followed the divine plan in our creation. He who is over all first gave us the right of choice. We are not machines wound up to run in certain grooves. God has given us power to choose between good and evil, between right and wrong. But we choose in this, as in temporal matters, evil or good, in electing the character of the government which is to be over us. The intelligent voter, in voting for President, takes into consideration the principles and tendency of the party represented, as well as the man who is its representative; for he knows that, in choosing the candidate, he chooses the party, and its principles and tendencies.

So there are placed before us candidates asking for our obedience and love, desiring to rule our hearts and lives. The Lord Jesus Christ stands before us as a candidate for our affection and trust. If we accept Him, we elect with Him all the gracious blessings of His government. We elect all the uplifting and ennobling influences of His Gospel. To choose Jesus is to choose all the fragrant fruits of spiritual living.

There is another candidate in the field. He appears under different disguises, in the same way that a political party sometimes so deftly arranges the planks of its platform that it appears different to different sections of the country. So the great party of evil presents its candidate to the human soul. But, after all, under all disguises, it is the same old candidate, whose name is Selfishness — to have one's own way, to indulge one's own appetites and passions, the lusts of the flesh. If we choose this candidate, we choose his party, and its principles and tendencies. We may resist them for a while, but ultimately they will assume real government over us. It is worth while knowing some of the people who are in this party. Paul, who was the greatest expositor of spiritual things, said, "The works of the flesh are manifest, which are these: fornication, uncleanness, lasciviousness, idolatry, sorcery, enmities, strife, jealousies, wraths, factions, divisions, heresies, envyings, drunkenness, revellings, and such like." None of this party ever gets to heaven. And surely there can be no conception of hell more terrible than to be perpetually under such a government.

On the other hand, the soul that chooses Jesus chooses His party, its principles and tendencies. The same great spiritual statesman whom I have quoted, says about it, "The fruit of the Spirit is love, joy, peace, long-suffering, kindness, goodness, faithfulness, meekness, temperance;" and Paul concludes that summary by saying, "They that are of Christ Jesus have crucified the flesh with the passions and the lusts thereof." What is that but saying that in the voting-place of one's own will — a place more secret and sacred than any Australian ballot system — a man has held an election, and chosen Jesus, and has out-voted and defeated utterly, and put to rout and confusion, all the opposition party of evil? When is the election day, do you ask? It may be now. "To-day is the day of salvation."

XX

JAMES RUSSELL LOWELL. THE POET-REFORMER.

JAMES RUSSELL LOWELL was a many-sided man, and there will be many to do him justice along all the lines where the force of his great character found expression. To me, however, first of all, and most of all, he was a great poet. He was a poet-preacher. Most of his poems are sermons in the highest sense, full of prophetic insight, sublime confidence in God and man, dauntless courage, and holy optimism that in spite of all discouragements and postponement sees ever the coming triumph of righteousness — qualities which belong to the true preacher.

Perhaps in our time there has been no more complete representative of New England ideas. He was the genius of Puritanism in our day.

It was Puritanism refined, cultivated, polished, but with all the old backbone of moral purpose and sterling integrity.

Lowell was poet not simply for the sake of the art. His muse was his pulpit. Great convictions stirred within him until they must find utterance, and found their most appropriate expression in verse. Behind everything he wrote, even in the most humorous passages of the "Biglow Papers," there was the blood-earnestness of a deep moral purpose. His conviction of a poet's duty is well expressed in these lines,—

> "He who would be the tongue of this wide land
>   Must string his harp with cords of sturdy iron,
> And strike it with a toil-embrowned hand."

One of the noblest triumphs of Lowell was that, though he was a member of an old and highly honorable family, born to learning and luxurious surroundings, he ever kept his sympathies fresh and in touch with the common people. For instance, he speaks like some earnest labor reformer when he says,—

> "Hard work is good and wholesome, past all doubt;
> But 'tain't so ef the mind gits tuckered out."

Or again in these lines, which are especially appropriate in these days of the "sweat shop," —

> " Slavery ain't o' nary color,
>   'Tain't the hide thet makes it wus,
>   All it keers fer in a feller
>   'S jest to make him fill its pus."

In a soberer way we find the same great lesson in that splendid parable where he represents the Christ as coming back to earth. He is given magnificent receptions on every hand by the wealthy and the high, and His images are pointed out to Him in the great churches everywhere, —

> " But still, wherever His steps they led,
>   The Lord in sorrow bent His head.
>   . . . .
>   Then Christ sought out an artisan,
>   A low-browed, stunted, haggard man,
>   And a motherless girl, whose fingers thin
>   Pushed from her faintly want and sin.
>
>   These He set in the midst of them,
>   And as they drew back their garment hem
>   For fear of defilement, ' Lo, here,' said He,
>   ' The images ye have made of Me!' "

But Lowell's sympathies were not only in touch with the people of his own land, of every class and station — his great heart overflowed the boundaries of State lines, and went out in earnest compassion to the suffering and oppressed of every land and tongue. How nobly this shines out in his song of the "Fatherland," —

> "Where'er a single slave doth pine,
>   Where'er one man may help another, —
>   Thank God for such a birthright, brother, —
> That spot of earth is thine and mine!
>   There is the true man's birthplace grand,
>   His is a world-wide fatherland!"

The mastery of duty was peculiarly illustrated in James Russell Lowell. No pharisaical feeling about the "filthy pool of politics" kept him back from doing sturdily what he deemed to be his duty as a citizen and a patriot. Through his life he was faithful to the conviction that, —

> "The day never comes when it'll du
>   To kick off duty like a worn-out shoe."

He was keenly sensitive to the needs of his own time, and had the soul of the prophet to detect the spirit of the age. He says, —

> " I sometimes think, the furder on I go,
> Thet it gits harder to feel sure I know;
> An' when I've settled my idees, I find
> 'Twarn't I sheered most in makin' up my mind;
> 'Twas this and thet an t'other thing thet done it,
> Sunthin' in th' air, I couldn' seek nor shun it."

He was also alert to the responsibility he was under to be faithful to each day's new duties, and felt that the treasures of the past were only held by those who were faithful to the opportunities of the present. —

> " Freedom gained yesterday is no more ours;
> Men gather but dry seeds of last year's flowers."

The two great anchorages of our humanity always held fast with Lowell. He had faith in man, —

> " An' thet's the old Amerikin idee,
> To make a man a Man, and let him be."

He had faith in God. To his thought, back of all the struggles of the race was the lofty purpose of God. How clearly this is shown in these oft-repeated words. —

> " Careless seems the great Avenger; . . .
> Truth forever on the scaffold, wrong forever on the throne;

> Yet that scaffold sways the future, and behind the dim unknown
> Standeth God within the shadow, keeping watch above His own."

Such a character as Lowell's could not but keep fresh and fruitful as the years went on. No one has detected more readily the emptiness of mere routine living, or warned us more sternly of the fatal loss of enthusiasm and generous spirit out of our human lives. How graphically has he set forth this danger in this sonnet of "The Street," —

> "They pass me by like shadows, crowds on crowds,
>   Dim ghosts of men, that hover to and fro,
> Hugging their bodies round them like thin shrouds
> Wherein their souls were buried long ago."

But the years in their flight left no dead soul's epitaph on Lowell's face. What he said of his friend Longfellow was realized in himself, —

> "Some suck up poison from a sorrow's core,
>   As naught but nightshade grew upon earth's ground;
> Love turned all his to heart's-ease, and the more
> Fate tried his bastions, she but forced a door
>   Leading to sweeter manhood and more sound."

XXI

WHITTIER AND THE GOLDEN RULE

WHAT public man, universally known through two generations, has stood so pre-eminently as the incarnation of the Golden Rule as John Greenleaf Whittier? The life has been as pure and as true as the songs. When Vice-President Henry Wilson was on his death-bed, he said, "If I had to do, to think, to act, and to vote just as I was directed by one man, I should choose Whittier. I believe him the purest man living on earth."

Whittier was the singing prophet of what was noblest in New England home, social, and civil life. In him the Puritan and Quaker blended into a harmonious manhood, which was at once both sweet and strong. He could speak the truth as sternly as Cromwell, but he spoke it in love as gentle and tender as a Quaker maiden's heart. His verse was the outflow of his noble Christian manhood. It is always earnest, sincere, sympathetic.

He was, throughout his life, under all emergencies, consistent to the true spirit of democracy. He held himself, —

> "Still to a stricken brother true,
>   Whatever clime hath nurtured him;
> As stooped to heal the wounded Jew,
>   The worshipper of Gerizim.
>
> By misery unrepelled, unawed
>   By pomp or power, thou seest a MAN
> In prince or peasant, — slave or lord, —
>   Pale priest, or swarthy artisan.
>
> Through all disguise, form, place, or name,
>   Beneath the flaunting robes of sin,
> Through poverty and squalid shame,
>   Thou lookest on *the man* within.
>
> On man, as man, retaining yet,
>   Howe'er debased, and soiled, and dim,
> A crown upon his forehead set, —
>   The immortal gift of God to him."

He judged everything by his standard of the Golden Rule, and was sensitive to detect any infringement of it. When he read that the clergy of all denominations had attended in a body a pro-slavery meeting, lending their sanction to its proceedings, he exclaimed,—

> "Just God! — and these are they
> Who minister at Thine altar, God of Right!
> Men who their hands with prayer and blessing lay
>   On Israel's Ark of light!
>
> What! preach, and kidnap men?
> Give thanks, — and rob Thy own afflicted poor?
> Talk of Thy glorious liberty, and then
>   Bolt hard the captive's door?"

But he was just as sensitive, on the other hand, to detect the spirit of the Golden Rule in unexpected places. When the story came home from the Mexican War that some noble Mexican women had cared for the hated Northern Yankees who were wounded on the battle-field with the same sympathy and tenderness bestowed on their own loved ones, his heart took fire and sang, —

> "Not wholly lost, O Father! is this evil world of ours;
>   Upward, through its blood and ashes, spring afresh the
>   Eden flowers;
>   From its smoking hell of battle, Love and Pity send
>   their prayer,
>   And still Thy white-winged angels hover dimly in our
>   air!"

The purse-proud atmosphere of the times never for a moment befogged his clear vision of the superiority of manhood to wealth. No rebuke was sterner than his when he saw, —

> "the dropping blood of labor
> Harden into gold;"

and beheld with tearful indignation, —

> "smooth-faced Mammon
> Reaping men like grain."

Defying the "Moloch in State Street," he declared, —

> "The gilded chambers built by wrong
> Invite the rust."

Whittier's ideal of a happy human life was in the realization of the Golden Rule, as will be seen from these lines, —

> "Released from that fraternal law
> Which shares the common bale and bliss,
> No sadder lot could Folly draw,
> Or Sin provoke from Fate, than this.
>
> The meal unshared is food unblessed;
> Thou hoard'st in vain what love should spend;
> Self-ease is pain; thy only rest
> Is labor for a worthy end."

And surely no man has written more in harmony with the spirit of Christ than in these verses from Whittier's hymn of "Worship,"—

> "O brother man! fold to thy heart thy brother;
>   Where pity dwells, the peace of God is there;
> To worship rightly is to love each other,
>   Each smile a hymn, each kindly deed a prayer.
>
> Follow with reverent step the great example
>   Of Him whose holy work was 'doing good;'
> So shall the wide earth seem our Father's temple,
>   Each loving life a psalm of gratitude."

XXII

LUCY LARCOM AND HER SWEET SONGS OF COMMON LIFE

LUCY LARCOM, of all American singers remaining with us at the time of her death, was pre-eminently the poet of common life. Born to toil, spending her early years in the factory, and thus knowing perfectly the trials and sorrows, as well as the joys and inspirations, of working people, she retained her fellowship and sympathy with them to the last. We have a window into the workshop, and into her own generous soul as well, in these verses from her song of "Weaving,"—

> "'I weave, and weave, the livelong day:
> The woof is strong, the warp is good:
> I weave, to be my mother's stay;
> I weave, to win my daily food:
> But ever as I weave,' saith she,
> 'The world of women haunteth me.
> . . . .

> 'I think of women sad and poor;
> Women who walk in garments soiled:
> Their shame, their sorrow, I endure;
> By their defect my hope is foiled:
> The blot they bear is on my name;
> Who sins, and I am not to blame?'"

American womanhood shows no more inspiring picture than Lucy Larcom in her "cloth-room," turning from her work at every spare moment during the day to her text-books on mathematics, grammar, English or German literature, which she kept on her desk. It is to her everlasting honor that, climbing upward by her own exertions, she retained that sweet spirit of sisterhood with all other toilers whom she had outstripped in the march of life by reason of her richer gifts.

I once knew a distinguished judge who had had no opportunities for early education, but who, after he was grown and married, by the aid of his indomitable will and tireless industry, so used his spare time while working as a country blacksmith, that he became well educated, mastered the law, and is now a celebrated United States judge. I heard this gentleman, in a public dining-room, bewail the fact, as one of the sad things in a democracy, that a gentleman's sons had to be educated in association with the boys from the homes of mechanics. How contemptible! Having climbed up himself by way of the forge and the anvil, he desired to close the ladder against all later comers.

There was nothing of this spirit about Lucy Larcom. She was ever the affectionate sister of the lowliest toiler. Her tender interpretation of the sorrows of the humble have caused the heart-strings of the whole world to vibrate. Her " Hannah Binding Shoes " has shared with Hood's " Song of the Shirt " in universal appreciation.

No one has sung more truly or more sweetly of the fellowship of humanity. The little dialogue of " Valley and Peak " illustrates this. —

" The Valley said to the Peak,
  'O Peak I fain would arise
And be great like you ! I would seek
  The wealth that illumes your skies!
Although I lie so low
  At your feet, I aspire to share
The splendor and strength you know,
  Lifted up into spacious air.'

> The Peak to the Valley said,
>   'O Valley, be content,
> Since for you my veins have bled,
>   And for you my breath is spent!
> Alone, for your sake, I live
>   In the cold and cloudy blue;
> Great only in that I give
>   The riches of heaven to you.' "

And no other poet has given us a finer expression of the great Scriptural revelation that it is "more blessed to give than to receive," —

> " Hand in hand with the angels;
>   Blessed so to be!
> Helped are all the helpers;
>   Giving light, they see.
> He who aids another
>   Strengthens more than one;
> Sinking earth he grapples
>   To the Great White Throne."

Or again, in the lines that follow, —

> " The secret of life, — it is giving;
>   To minister and to serve;
> Love's law binds the man to the angel,
>   And ruin befalls, if we swerve."

Lucy Larcom came into such close touch with the humblest human lives, that she knew of the hidden vein of precious metal that many do not see, and, failing to perceive, come to be sceptical as to its existence. There are many in these great cities who, lost in the whirl of business success, forget the immortal values that are at stake in lives that hang on their forbearance or generosity. All such need to pray Lucy Larcom's prayer in the poem entitled "The Stray Leaf," —

> "Dear Father, Thy handwriting make us see
> On each soiled fragment of humanity!"

And we all need to learn that there can be no real acceptance of Jesus Christ as our own Saviour without a true appreciation of the universal brotherhood. How truly she sings it! —

> "Not my Christ only; He is ours;
> Humanity's close bond."

In this age, so permeated with a sceptical materialism, it is refreshing to catch the spirit of this noble woman's cheerful faith. She believed with Phillips Brooks that the greatest of all revelations of God is that which He makes to the individual soul. Hence she says, —

"'Tis the Eternal Deep that answers to the deep within my soul."

And yet again, —

> " He cheats not any soul. He gave
> Each being unity like His;
> Love, that links beings, He must save;
> Of Him it is."

To her He was the

> "Life, that breathest in all sweet things
> That bud and bloom upon the earth,
> That fillest the sky with songs and wings."

And sometimes in the hurry of prosaic city life heavenly vision was given to her, as to Paul on his way to Damascus, —

> "I cannot tell how, yet I know it, —
> That once unto me it was given,
> 'Mid the noonday stir of the city,
> To breathe for a moment of heaven.
>
> The heaven that is hidden within us
> For a moment was open to me,
> And I caught a glimpse of the glory
> That perhaps we might always see."

One who opens the heart to God like that can always summon one's own self, as she did, to lofty work. In that splendid poem, "A Word with My Soul," she says, —

> "Build up, Soul, a lofty stair;
> Build a room in healthier air!
>   Here there is no rest:
>   Better climbs to best.
> Thy friends shall be the eternal stars;
> They greet thee through thy casement bars:
>   Thy homesick feet they lead
>   Where thou no house wilt need."

A soul having such a consciousness of itself and of its God can have no fear about its immortality.

> "The living soul spells not the name of death."

And who has so sweetly described those blessed premonitions of the life to come which all earnest souls have shared?

> "Odors from blossoming worlds unknown
> Across my path are blown;
> Thy robes trail hither myrrh and spice
> From farthest Paradise;
> I walk through Thy fair universe with Thee,
> And sun me in Thine immortality."

XXIII

THE YACHT RACE AS A PICTURE OF HUMAN LIFE

"The swift ships." — Job ix. 26.

A YACHT race, with the world for an audience, has been the wholesome spice in the past week's making of history. Any new illustration of the power of man to lord it over the forces of nature is sure of a hearing; and when to this is added national spirit in earnest rivalry, the interest is intensified. But the ship is used so often in the Bible to point a moral, or teach a serious lesson, that we ought not to let this universal interest in swift ships go by without seeking to gather from them some lessons that will remain with us when all this ephemeral enthusiasm shall have passed away.

Each one of our human lives has many points of resemblance to a ship; and in soul navigation many of the experiences jotted down in a ship's logbook are reproduced.

As I have read the reports of the preparations for the international yacht race, the first thing that has impressed me has been that much depended upon the model of the vessel — a failure there would doom the swift ship from the beginning. The timber that is to enter into the construction of the vessel, and all other materials, must be of the very best; and the model must be as near perfection as human ingenuity can devise. No one has painted the building of a ship so well as our own Longfellow, —

> "In the shipyard stood the Master,
>   With the model of the vessel,
> That should laugh at all disaster,
>   And with wave and whirlwind wrestle!
>
> Covering many a rood of ground,
> Lay the timber piled around;
> Timber of chestnut, and elm, and oak,
> And scattered here and there, with these,
> The knarred and crooked cedar knees;
> . . . .
> Ah! what a wondrous thing it is
> To note how many wheels of toil
> One thought, one word, can set in motion!

> There's not a ship that sails the ocean,
> But every climate, every soil,
> Must bring its tribute great or small,
> And help to build the wooden wall!"

How like that is to the building of a man or woman; especially in our day when the world is brought into such close fellowship. Not only is every land put under tribute, but every age in the world's history. No geologist has ever delved in the rocks, no astronomer ever peered into the Milky Way, no poet ever sung, no warrior ever led the soldiers of freedom, no orator ever stirred the noble ambitions of his fellows, no martyr ever suffered at the stake or on the cross, but they contribute, one and all, in intelligence or liberty, to the making of the soul that is building in our midst to-day.

The ship in its early stage of building shows little of the beauty which is disclosed after a while, when, with all sails flying, it rides upon the wave like some great celestial bird — "a thing of life." Let us look through Longfellow's lines again.—

> "Day by day the vessel grew,
> With timbers fashioned strong and true,
> Stemson and keelson and sternson-knee,
> Till, framed with perfect symmetry,

A skeleton ship rose up to view !
And around the bows and along the side
The heavy hammers and mallets plied,
Till after many a week, at length,
Wonderful for form and strength,
Sublime in its enormous bulk,
Loomed aloft the shadowy hulk !
And around it columns of smoke, upwreathing,
Rose from the boiling, bubbling, seething
Caldron, that glowed,
And overflowed
With the black tar, heated for the sheathing ;
And amid the clamors
Of clattering hammers,
He who listened heard now and then
The song of the Master and his men : —
' Build me straight, O worthy Master,
   Stanch and strong, a goodly vessel,
That shall laugh at all disaster,
   And with wave and whirlwind wrestle ! ' "

Much of the discipline of youth is like the noise of the hammers and the smell of boiling tar. That need not discourage us if only the young life is being formed after the true model, and wrought upon by skilful and honest hands. The most discouraging thing one sees in the great human dockyards is that so many ships seem to be thrown together without plan or model. Many put to sea only painted hulls, having seemed to care for nothing save galley and bunk; and, without rudder, mast, or sail, drift from the beginning, the plaything of every chance tide that sweeps the ocean of human life.

Another thing that has interested me is that the greatest care has been exercised over these fast yachts to see that they were in perfect condition for the race. They were taken out of the water, everything scraped off, and the copper sheathing smoothed, so that not even the slightest wrinkle should retard the swift motion of the vessel. Every stick of timber, and every yard of sail, was carefully gone over, that there might be no doubt that they were strong enough to bear the great strain that might come upon them, and not be found wanting in the moment of emergency. And we know this was wise; for in the great English races, recently, a race was lost by a rotten sail.

How plain is the lesson taught us by these careful preparations for a few miles of exciting rivalry! With these immortal souls we are sailing a voyage of infinite importance. We are sailing on an ocean where the "soft south winds" may be suddenly displaced by the wild fury of "Euroclydon." We should carefully fit ourselves for life's voyage. Carefulness will mean all the difference between a prosperous voyage and a safe port, or the bottom of the ocean, or a vessel broken on the rocks.

How many there are in life's race who drift out of the track of successful vessels, with a broken mast or a torn sail! How many become water-logged, and the inspiration of the voyage is lost by the cruel work at the pumps to keep the vessel afloat! How earnest are the orders of our Captain, "Watch and pray, lest ye enter into temptation." Again and again that command to be alert and vigilant was rung out on the disciples' ears.

In Isaiah a wicked man is compared to a ship whose tacklings are loosed. Of course a ship whose tacklings are loosed from her masts is not fit for service and is in constant peril. No intelligent sailor would consent to sail on such a ship. But we meet men and women every day who are out on the serious voyage of human life with the gearing of mind and heart all loose. In fine weather, when everything is propitious, they make no headway, and at the first severe storm they are cast away. The beautiful Gitana, which once led the yachts of the world, under the skilful management of Captain Sherlock, falling into careless hands, was stranded on the rocks. Sad as it is to see a stranded ship, it does not compare with a stranded man or woman with sails flapping helplessly against the mast, out of life's channel and beached beyond hope.

A yacht trimmed for the race must be clear of every hindrance; so if we will make swift progress in the divine life, we must "lay aside every weight, and the sin which doth so easily beset us." Have you never seen a vessel down the harbor, when the tide was running out, swinging with it, and seeming as if it would follow that ocean call, yet could not because of the hidden anchor whose flukes were imbedded in the deep mud of the bay? So many a soul is drawn by the heavenly currents; and ever and anon as the tides of their better self surge about them they sway that way, but yet always fall back again to wallow in the harbor, because they are anchored to some secret sin which holds them fast.

Another fact about yachting has been especially emphasized this past week. That is that the ship must be propelled by some power foreign to herself. If she have no engine to generate steam, then she must spread her sails, and depend upon the wind; and if that fails, as it did last Thursday, the race becomes only a drift. So this ship of the immortal soul needs the heavenly trade-winds, the wind of the Spirit, to speed her on her way. Many times we fail to make progress because we do not spread the canvas to catch the breeze offered us. One of the captains, this past week, was criticised by the newspapers (who always know how to sail a boat, or conduct a lawsuit, or preach a sermon, better than does the captain or judge or preacher) because he did not manage to get the full benefit of the little movement there was in the air. Whether that were just or not, we all know that in the higher realms of spiritual navigation a vast amount of power remains unused.

Some one writing about steamships recently,

said that one of the great scientific problems of the age is how to utilize steam so as to gain the full value of it. In a locomotive or an ocean liner only a comparatively small percentage of the steam can at present be brought to bear upon the propelling agent. The remainder goes to waste. Much the same thing is true in the realm of religious achievement. Only a portion of our spiritual powers and opportunities are fully used. One of the most pressing needs of the cause of Christ upon earth is that those who profess to have it at heart should give it the benefit of the full exercise of their powers and opportunities. Were no other advance than this to be made during the coming year, the world, and probably the church also, would be amazed by the improved state of things which would result.

How can this desirable object be obtained? The first step naturally is for every Christian to ask this question, "What spiritual possibilities am I personally allowing to remain neglected or imperfectly used?" To answer this question honestly will lead most of us to a more conscientious study of ourselves, which in itself will be of great and permanent benefit. There will be few, if indeed there be any, who cannot thus discover directions in which they can and ought to consecrate themselves individually more earnestly to the Divine service, and to put forth more wise and zealous efforts for the religious good of others. We will not dwell now upon the duty of endeavoring to grow in grace. This is obvious and conceded. Assuming it, and the more fully because an increase of devotedness to God in the form of effort made for others always results in an increase of the consecration of the worker, we would put emphasis on the duty of trying to discover what more we can do than we are doing to commend Christ and His truth to others by service rendered them.

The way to test a ship is to give her a chance at the breeze, with the blue waves under her keel. As Henry Ward Beecher once said, Suppose a man should sail, all the boiling and blazing day, round and round a ship in the harbor; and the next day you should see him, like a magnified fly, creeping up and down the masts and spars, and examining the rigging: and you should ask him what he was doing, and he should answer, "I have heard that this ship is a dull sailer, and I want to look and see." Could he ever find out that way? No. Let him weigh anchor and spread canvas, and take the wind and bear away, if he would know how she sails.

So if a Christian would learn his true state, let him not row gloomily around the hull of his self-consciousness, and creep with morbid egotism up and down the masts and spars of his feelings and affections, but let him spread the sails of resolution and bear away on the ocean of duty.

There is one thing in which this spiritual race in which we are all entered differs from the international yacht race. In that only one can win the prize, but in the higher race all may win. And because my brother's ship passes rapidly on I am not delayed; for sometimes in a race one yacht, by getting ahead in a certain position, will take a rival's wind, and so retard it. Thank God that in soul navigation the prosperity of one makes it easier for every one else! All envy, therefore, is not only sin, but the greatest folly; and we ought to hail with brotherliness every passing ship on life's stormy main. As ships meet at sea and signal a word of greeting to each other, and grant help when needed, so men meet in this world; and we ought not to cross any man's path without hailing him, and, if he needs, give him supplies. As, —

"Ships that pass in the night, and speak each other in passing,
Only a signal shown and a distant voice in the darkness;
So, on the ocean of life we pass and speak one another,
Only a look and a voice, then darkness again and a silence."

Do you remember the wave of enthusiasm that swept over this country a few years ago, when that brave Philadelphia captain threw overboard his costly cargo that he might make room for the sinking Norwegian steamship? So we ought always to be ready to unload earthly treasures, if thereby we may give succor to brother ships sailing for immortal climes.

But after all else has been done, the vessel must be in the hands of a safe pilot. How many promising human ships are being wrecked these days through that fatal lack! O my brother, do not sail without the Great Pilot at the helm! He will guide us safe through life's storms, and past all dangers, safe into the haven at last.

Tennyson sang, —

> "Sunset and evening star,
>   And one clear call for me!
> And may there be no moaning of the bar,
>   When I put out to sea.
>
> But such a tide as moving seems asleep,
>   Too full for sound and foam.
> When that which drew from out the boundless deep
>   Turns again home.
>
> Twilight and evening bell,
>   And after that the dark!
> And may there be no sadness of farewell,
>   When I embark;
>
> For tho' from out our bourn of Time and Place,
>   The flood may bear me far,
> I hope to see my Pilot face to face
>   When I have crost the bar."

Sweet as that is, some one else sings, with more of spiritual assurance and insight, this prayer to Christ. —

"Be Thou my Guide on life's tempestuous sea;
    Be Thou my Guide.
The waves run high, and all seems dark to me;
    Be Thou my Guide.
Take Thou the helm, and steer me safely o'er
Life's surging sea to the celestial shore.

I did not always fear that winds or sea
    Could overwhelm:
I never looked, I never prayed to Thee
    To take the helm.
I trusted to myself through storm and wave,
And never thought of Him who came to save.

I tried to do without Thee, but in vain —
    In vain the hope;
With all the perils of the 'whelming main
    I could not cope;
Now from the deep I turn my eyes to Thee;
O Saviour, take the helm and pilot me!"

XXIV

A CROWN FOR THE MAN WHO FAILS

"Among them that are born of women there is none greater than John." — LUKE vii. 28 (R.V.).

"And she went out, and said unto her mother, What shall I ask? And she said, The head of John the Baptist." — MARK vi. 24 (R.V.).

THESE two brief Scriptures place before us two pictures in the life of a strong and interesting man. In the first one we have the testimony of the best judge of human nature that ever walked among men; He who more perfectly than anybody else knew what was in man. This competent judge, speaking to the multitudes that thronged about Him, declared that John was as great a man as ever lived. And yet it is only a few days thereafter that we see the head of this great man coming into the palace dining-room on a charger, as a prize to a thoughtless dancing-girl, to appease the vengeance of her dissolute and vindictive mother. To the superficial observer the life of John seems to have ended in failure. All his ministry of promise, and it had promised much, is broken down at what seems to be the opening of a great career. To our short-sighted judgment no one could have been so well fitted to be the chief apostle of the new faith as the man who with such simplicity and fidelity and such dauntless courage had proclaimed the coming of the Christ. He is still a young man, scarcely entering on middle life. His best years ought to be yet before him. But all this promise of a career of greatness, which is enhanced by the sublime words of appreciation of Jesus Himself, is eclipsed by the darkness of the dungeon, and finally destroyed by the executioner's axe. And yet we all feel that the life of John the Baptist was not a failure, that rather it was a great and splendid success. For more than eighteen hundred years poor old Herod has been dethroned — a corrupt, beggarly outcast by the universal verdict of public opinion; and John has been enthroned as a true and noble character who filled well his mission.

Surely there must be more than appears on the surface of life if this is so.

Now, John is only an illustration of what is going on constantly among men and women in every walk of life. There are many people with honest hearts and good purposes, who are faithful to God and their duty, loving their fellows, and yet their lives fail of the usual crown of devotion and toil, and they are cut down just as the blossom is beginning to bud upon their tree of promise. Some men fight and win. They are crowned with glory. All the way along they are cheered by sympathetic multitudes and followed by applause. Others, just as true, fight as faithfully, only to be defeated and forgotten of men. Now, the whole spirit of our Bible and our Christianity is full of consolation and comfort for people who fight honestly for the right, and, so far as the world can see, fail.

Walt Whitman writes in that strange style of his, which, however, is not strange enough to hide the true poetic insight into human nature which it discloses, a song for the men who fail. —

"With music strong I come, with my cornets and my drums;
I play not marches for accepted victors only,
I play marches for conquered and slain persons.
Have you heard that it was good to gain the day?
I also say it is good to fall; battles are lost in the same
 spirit in which they are won.
I beat and pound for the dead,
I blow through my embouchures my loudest and gayest
 for them;
Vivas to those who have failed!
And to those whose war vessels sank in the sea!
And to those themselves who sank in the sea!
And to all generals that lost engagements, and all over-
 come heroes!
And the numberless unknown heroes equal to the greatest
 heroes known!
Did we think victory great?
So it is; but now it seems to me . . . that defeat is great,
And that death and dismay are great."

Christ gave a marvellous illustration of how easy it is for men to blunder in their estimate of what constitutes success and failure in His story of Dives and Lazarus. Everybody thought Dives was a prosperous man. And, no doubt, all were just as unanimous that Lazarus was a most miserable failure. Perhaps even the street curs who licked his sores had a contempt for the poor wretch who could not drive them away. And yet in the eye of the

All-Wise Judge, Dives was a failure, and Lazarus was a conspicuous success. I wonder if some of us are not making the same mistake in our judgments now.

In Beatrice Harraden's brilliant book, "Ships that Pass in the Night," there is given a unique and interesting little parable in which the Genius of Failure and the Genius of Success passed away from earth together, and found themselves in a foreign land. Success still wore her laurel wreath which she had worn on earth. There was a look of ease about her whole appearance, and there was a smile of pleasure and satisfaction on her face as though she knew she had done well, and had deserved her honors. Failure's head was bowed; no laurel wreath encircled it; her wan face bore traces of pain. She had once been beautiful and hopeful, but both hope and beauty had been lost in sorrow and disappointment. They stood together, these two who differed so widely in their appearance, waiting for an audience with the sovereign of the foreign land. Finally an old gray-haired man came to them and asked their names.

"I am Success," said Success, advancing a step forward and smiling at him as she pointed to her laurel wreath.

He shook his head.

"Ah," he said, "do not be too confident. Very often things go by opposite names in this land. What you call Success we often call Failure, and what you call Failure we call Success. Do you see these two men waiting there? The one nearer to us was thought to be a good man in your world. The other was generally accounted bad; but here we call the bad man good, and the good man bad. That seems strange to you. Well, then, look yonder. You considered that statesman to be sincere; but we say he was insincere. We chose as our poet-laureate a man at whom your world scoffed. Ay, and those flowers yonder: for us they have a fragrant charm; we love to see them near us. But you do not even take the trouble to pluck them from the hedges where they grow in rich profusion. So, you see, what we value as a treasure, you do not value at all."

Then he turned to Failure.

"And your name?" he asked kindly.

"I am Failure," she said sadly.

He took her by the hand.

"Come, now, Success," he said to her, "let me lead you into the Presence-Chamber."

Then she who had been called Failure, and was now called Success, lifted up her bowed head, and raised her weary frame, and smiled at the music of her new name. And with that smile she regained her beauty and her hope. And hope having come back to her, all her strength returned.

I wonder if Lazarus had an experience like that when the angels bore him in triumph to Abraham's bosom.

Many a splendid success is built upon the heroic failures that have gone before. A mining expert who was recently sent to investigate some Arizona properties for Denver capitalists, on his return reported the finding of a most remarkable natural bridge formed by a tree of agatized wood, spanning a cañon forty-five feet in width. The tree had at some remote time fallen and become imbedded in the slip of some great inland sea or mighty water overflow. The slip became in time sandstone, and the wood gradually passed through the stages of mineralization until it became a wonderful tree of solid agate. In after years the water washed away the sandstone until the cañon was formed; and the flint-like substance of the agatized wood having resisted the erosion, it remained to form the bridge. Where the bark has been broken and torn away from the trunk of the tree, the characteristic colors of jasper and agate are seen. To the naked eye the wood is beautiful, but under a miner's magnifying glass the brilliancy of the colorings is clearly brought out in all their wondrous beauty. So many a life tree, prostrated and forgotten, comes to be the beautiful bridge over which the future generations walk to triumph. An English poet sings, —

"Failed? 'Ah, yes, poor fellow!' you say.
   'Nothing from life he seemed to gain.
His was a truly losing fight,
And all too soon the cruel night
    Closed around — beat him down. He was slain.
      Yes, failed,' you say.

Failed! But I tell you, tell you, Nay!
   'Twas a noble fight he fought, and well —

With courage held high and brow clear,
No skulking idly in the rear,
  And if vanquished, 'twere fighting — fighting he
  fell.
   No failure, I say.

And look you! What call you success?
  The poor plaudits of some few men?
A palace reared from the cold —
A red heap of this earth-dug gold?
  A cathedral crypt? And then — well what then?
   Why, only a guess.

And I say again, Count you the cost
  Of this bridge? To what is it nailed?
What are its bulwarks piled high — these
You cross to the city of ease?
  Man, I tell you 'tis built on the failed —
   The fighters who lost.

And he — scorn or pity as you will —
  'Twas fording that stream he fell.
For Freedom, for Man, for the Right!
Was his cry in the heat of the fight;
  And for these, and for you, rang his knell.
   Then, 'failed' say you still?

Dry-shod reach your Promised Land now
  On his failure — on those the world railed —
They, the stuff of whom heroes are,
Who saw its lights gleam from valleys afar,
  And fought for it — died for it — failed.
   No failure, I vow."

The common soil of human life is constantly producing fragrant flowers of heroism and self-sacrifice for the exhibition of which saints and martyrs and heroes have been crowned; yet for every romantic and splendid deed which has succeeded in gaining immortal honor among men, there are ten thousand actions just as beautiful that go unsung.

One of the New York daily papers only this week contained the story of a Hungarian whose wife has been ill at the Bellevue Hospital. The other morning he walked several miles to the hospital, carrying in his arms an eighteen months' old baby boy and a few pieces of stale bread, which in his ignorance he thought his wife needed. He was found staggering about like a drunken man outside the walls of the hospital. When brought in, both he and the babe seemed in a sort of stupor. Finally he managed to make the warden understand that neither himself nor child had eaten anything for three days. The warden sent for some milk. It was offered to the babe, who was too weak to swallow at first, but finally managed to drink. When the milk was offered to the father he declined to accept it, saying his share should be given to the baby; and the noble fellow, though he was starving, would not touch it until he was assured that the child should have all the nourishment it wanted. To my mind the story of Sir Philip Sidney and his glass of water on the battle-field does not reveal a nobler quality of soul than that possessed by this poor Hungarian.

On a train going into Philadelphia the other day a party of fashionable young people, who had been out to a club-house picnic, filled the cars. They were all of this class with the exception of one tired, faded-looking old woman, who carried in her arms a bundle done up in a newspaper — a loosely tied, slip-shod package that she handled with care. When the crowd surged into the car she took her seat at the extreme end, in one of the places that brought her right in the midst of a group of particularly wild and gay young revellers. With anxious care she held on her lap the package done up in its greasy paper, and ever and anon a tear-drop fell on it. A lurch of the train threw one of the young fellows, who was sitting on the arm of the seat, almost on to the precious bundle. With a startled exclamation, and voice made shrill by fear, the woman cried, —

"Look out! Can't you see you are crushing the bundle?"

"I beg ten thousand pardons, madam," replied the youth, who, owing to his awkward lurch and the sharp exclamation of the woman, had raised a laugh at his expense. "Won't you allow me to secure you a seat in the baggage-car, where you and your trunk will be in no danger of being harmed by contact with the wide world?" And in an undertone he added to his companions, "It's the place for cattle, anyhow. The English system of first, second, and third class is far superior to our mode of crowding in with all sorts of creatures."

The quick ear of the woman had caught the word "cattle," and she sprang to her feet like a tigress.

"Cattle, is it!" she exclaimed. "I may not be a lady like your pretty friend, but I am a woman, with a woman's feelings. That bundle has flowers in it for me dead baby. While yez were dancin' and drinkin', me little boy was lyin' cold and stiff, and these two arms, that should have held him, had to wash the dishes at the club-house to get money enough to take me back to the day nursery where I left him this mornin'. I have known me little boy was dead for four hours; and with me heart breakin' I had to go on with me work to get me money. There's only a few buttercups in that bundle; but me little boy loved them, and I mane to carry them to where he is, and place them in the little dead hands and around the little body. Oh, me baby! me baby!"

And the poor mother, overcome by her feelings, sank into her seat and gave way for the first time to an unrestrained fit of sobbing and crying that shook her frame and left not a dry eye in the car. To my mind, history does not hold a more poetic vision of mother-love than is revealed in that poor old Irishwoman and her bundle of buttercups for her dead baby.

Harvard College has just received a very remarkable gift. A colored woman, Harriet Hayden, escaped from slavery before the war, and found refuge with her husband and baby in Canada. During the Rebellion her heart went out in prayerful longings to help her own poor people, and she came to be acquainted with Governor Andrew of Massachusetts, and was of great assistance to him in enlisting negro soldiers. This woman has just paid into the treasury of Harvard College, out of her own hard work, a scholarship fund of five thousand dollars, the annual income of which is to be used perpetually to aid each year some deserving colored student. There are no scales on earth fine enough to weigh a gift like that, or to measure the sacrifices and tears and prayers and holy devotion that have gone into the saving of that five thousand dollars. I can imagine Jesus standing by at the treasury as of old, and looking at all the gifts of hundreds and thousands of millions as they came into the treasury of education last year, and I can hear Him say, as this poor old black woman hobbles up on her crutch with her bag of savings, "She hath given more than they all." The world may count her life a failure, but it will shine out through the great eternities as a marvellous success.

The eleventh chapter of Hebrews, which

is called sometimes the roll-call of the heroes of the faith, has also been aptly called an "Epic of Failure:" for it is from beginning to end a glorification of men who were foiled and defeated. Abraham, Isaac, Jacob, Joseph, Moses, and multitudes of others who were just as faithful and true, but whose names were not even gathered for history's urn, although the world was not worthy of them, walked not by sight but by faith, lived ever in hope of the promise, and yet all died without entering into the promised land which they longed for. They all achieved their final victory by failure. And when we come for our final illustration to Him who is at once our Saviour and our Exemplar, the Christ, what more conspicuous lesson of His life than that great triumph cannot be had except at the cost of failure? The very mob that surrounded His cross shouted this in His dying face when they said, "He saved others, Himself He cannot save." To human judgment no life ever ended in such conspicuous failure as that of Jesus Christ: and yet it is the only life that has reached a perfect success. How absolute the failure seemed on that day

of the crucifixion! Christ seemed given over
to the power of His enemies. Suppose you
had stood in that street in Jerusalem, in front
of Pilate's judgment hall, and watched as the
howling mob came pouring out after the final
decision. And as you watch the poor, friendless man fainting beneath His cross, you say
to yourself, "Alas! is this, too, a failure?
I had hoped that this man might have brought
redemption. As I have listened to His wonderful words, and caught the heavenly tones
of love in His voice, and looked on His
mighty works, I have hoped that here might
be the Divine Personage who was to bring
salvation to the race. But, alas, He, too,
has failed! What a pitiful end for what
promised so much!" And if, as you thus
meditated aloud, some proud Jew, perchance
a member of the Sanhedrin, had overheard
you, and you had turned to him with your
question, "Where, oh, where is the secret
balm that is to heal the heart-aches of the
world and lift mankind up to righteousness and
real triumph?" he would have pointed you to
the temple, and said, "In yonder temple. In

the Jewish faith and religion is the world's greatest power, and it shall yet triumph over all." And if as you listened to him some bright-eyed Greek had passed that way, and you had turned to him with your question, he would have replied, "Have you been at Athens? Have you listened to her philosophers? Have you looked on her paintings and her sculpture? In Grecian art and learning is hidden the world's most splendid force." And if while you listened to him some proud Roman soldier had come along with martial tread, and you had made your inquiry, he would have said, "Have you been in Rome? She is to be the eternal city. Have you seen her magnificent armies? Have you studied her grand and simple laws? In Roman force and organization is the mighty power which is to make all the earth bow before her triumphant eagles." And if you had pointed them to that poor, despised, condemned maker of parables, and said, "You are all wrong: the simple words of that poor prisoner there will outlive your temple or your sculpture or your armies; that despised man, fainting under His cross, is the mightiest force in the world," how they would have laughed you to scorn. But the centuries go by, and Roman and Grecian and Jewish civilizations are swept away like chaff before the wind in the summer's harvest-field, and the crucified failure from Nazareth fills the earth with His power, and counts the armies of His devoted soldiery by hundreds of millions!

With such failure and such triumph before us we can afford to do our duty and leave the result to God.

XXV

THE COMING OF CHRIST'S KINGDOM IN NEW YORK CITY

An address delivered at the twenty-eighth anniversary of the New York City Church Extension and Missionary Society held in Madison Avenue M. E. Church, April 24, 1894.

MR. PRESIDENT.—I am glad to see this little note [referring to the summary on the programme] in the next to the last line on the bottom of the page that records these "important facts." The appeal is to the people "who believe in the coming of Christ's kingdom in New York city."

I tell you, brothers and sisters, that right along that line is where we lack real belief. A faith that Christ does intend to rule in New York city and Brooklyn and Boston and Chicago—real faith that is alive and active, that the cities are to become the kingdoms of our Christ—I believe we lack that more than anything else. We will have victory when the church comes really to believe that the cities are to become the kingdoms of Christ. I had occasion to say, a few Sunday mornings ago, something about the duty of the church to conquer the city, and the next day some one sent me anonymously a tract, the substance of which was that the city was a mere fire-trap for the devil, and that all we could expect to do was to pick out a burning brand here and there and save it. Now, I tell you, friends, there is a good deal of that sort of scepticism in the church. That miserable little tract represents the lack of faith of a large number of our people. Miserable proverbs we make about the "city being made by man," etc.; and all of it covering up a sort of belief that somehow the city is contrary to divine order. We get it into our heads that a city is a bad thing in itself; but undoubtedly we are on the verge of greater cities yet. The last generation or two seems a miracle to us, and yet we are on the verge of greater cities. The legislation already gone through, preparing the way for greater New York and greater Boston and greater Cleveland, is an index finger that points as sure as can be to the fact that we are on the threshold of greater cities than the world has ever seen. And undoubtedly the city is in God's order and God's providence, and the cities must rule very largely the destinies of the future in the State and nation. What a marvellous mastery it has to-day! In the very nature of things it must continue to have this mastery. The great business houses are here in the city, and they dictate standards of trade and trade morals throughout the whole country everywhere. The great newspapers and publishing-houses are here, and all the great forces that make public sentiment and the standards of public opinion, that make and master the country — these are in the cities; and we must master the cities or we might as well give up the situation entirely.

The programme of the Christian Church must include the possession and the occupation of the cities in the name of the Lord Jesus Christ. We must make up our minds to that, and we must believe for it. Now, I believe thoroughly that it is just as easy to win men to Christ to-day as it ever has been in the history of the world. I don't think there has ever been a time when the depraved human heart has not revolted against the tender, loving purity of the Lord Jesus Christ — when it has not been necessary that the wicked heart should yield itself in surrender to the Lord Jesus Christ. There has always been the same opposition to Christianity that there is to-day, in substance. Christianity has won, where it has won, because it has been presented by warm, loving hearts full of faith in the Holy Ghost. When there has been the earnest contact of the living messenger with living men, the people have surrendered to Christ. What we need is that in the pulpit and in the pew the people shall believe that we are in these cities to win them for the Lord Jesus Christ. I think there is nothing more shameful and nothing more sorrowful than the cowardice of the Christian people, many times exemplified in our cities by their attitude toward public life. We all know very well (and I know these are commonplaces that I say for a moment, yet they need to be said over again in times like this) that there are enough Christian men in the United States to take this infamous liquor traffic by the throat and shake it to death as a dog shakes the life out of a rat. And yet we go on and let it rule and master us, permitting it to sit in places of power. You know there are Christian men enough in New York City to shake Tammany Hall to death, and yet we let it go on with its open corruption. We know very well there are Christian men and women enough in these great cities to put Christian men in the places of power, in the mayor's chair and the high offices of authority, and yet we somehow sit calmly back and let the thing go on, and let the devil come into mastery and power in our great cities.

Now, what we need is a real faith — a faith that the Lord Jesus Christ has power to conquer these cities, and He will conquer them if we do our duty, and if we go forth as His disciples with our faces bathed with courage and our hearts clothed as the sons and daughters of the Most High God. I believe it is possible to have Pentecost in our modern cities to-day. I believe it with all my heart. And wherever you show me men and women with the divine daring of early Christianity in Jerusalem, pressing face to face, hand to hand, shoulder to shoulder, the same preaching, the same praying, the same believing, I will show you the same sort of work. Over in Boston we have had during the past few months a devoted Italian missionary, a young man with the daring of the hundred and twenty men and women at Pentecost, preaching, in his own tongue, the story of the crucifixion and resurrection; and that city saw more Roman Catholics converted to Jesus Christ, and born to Methodist Christianity, this year, than in all our Italian Missions. I do not say that critically of our Italian missionaries — nothing of the sort — but this shows that our cities have possibilities in them beyond anything we ever dreamed about.

We are on the very eve of great revivals among these foreign peoples in our midst. All our cities to-day are in the same condition that Jerusalem was in on the day of Pentecost when the disciples went out to preach. One of the astonishing things then was that every man heard the Gospel in his own tongue. They talked to the people face to face with burning hearts and burning words, and men were persuaded to cry, "What shall we do to be saved?" We have people of every nationality, every tribe, every kindred and tongue; and I am glad to see in these "important facts" that you are preaching the Gospel in a number of languages. We ought to-day to be preaching the Gospel in every language that is spoken in our streets, and we ought to get close to the people and preach to them in their own tongue. I am afraid there are tens of thousands of people who speak English who don't get the Gospel in their own tongue. When you preach to a man in his own tongue, it means that you are going to get alongside of him on the plane of brotherhood and look straight into a brother's eyes, and tell him of a Christ who has redeemed your soul and given you the hope of glory and of immortal life. And that is what we need to do in these cities all about us, among the rich and among the poor. We need to feel down in the depths of our hearts, in every one of our churches, that all of these people — the poorest of them, and the wickedest and most depraved and criminal among them — that they are the sons and daughters of God, the brothers and sisters of the Lord Jesus Christ; that they are dear to the heart of God, and that He loves them as tenderly as we love our little children. There must be no more caste for us than there was for Jesus Christ. I know that many of these people are very bad. Many of them are degraded and seem to be incapable of higher feeling. I have worked too much among what are called the very poorest people in the cities not to understand these things that seem to stand in the way.

Old Father Taylor, of the Seamen's Church, used to say that there are three kinds of people in the world — the Lord's poor, the devil's poor, and the poor devils. We have got along to the point in most of our churches where, if a man can show an orthodox pedigree for three or four generations, and can prove himself as one of the Lord's poor, we will have some sort of sympathy for him, and give him some sort of tenderness and brotherhood. But I want to know, my brother, who is going to look after the devil's poor and the poor devils? We don't get that sneer for either one of those classes from our Master. Our Saviour was as full of sympathy and tenderness for that poor fellow over among the tombs of Gadara as He was with anybody else He had to deal with during the whole course of His ministry. I tell you that these depraved people, the people out of whom we are constantly filling our jails and our penitentiaries — these people are the brothers and sisters of the Lord Jesus Christ; and no matter how poor and degraded and sinful, whatever you do for them, Christ has promised that He will receive it as though it were done for Him. And in the worst there is this great fact, that they are the sons and daughters of the great God. He grieves over them and longs to see them saved; and is as happy, and the angels are as happy, when they are reclaimed, as if one of the richest men in New York were converted. These "devil's poor" are just as good as the "devil's rich;" and we must get it into our hearts that there are none of them, rich or poor, who rightfully belong to Satan, but God wants them saved. The devil is an invading enemy, and they belong to God. They may be covered over with sin and sorrow and with degradation, but they are God's children; and there are possibilities in every one of them of being won to wholesomeness and healthfulness and everlasting glory.

I tell you the finest things that men have ever written about the possibilities of reclaiming men can more than be equalled by actual facts. Sometimes people think that the story of Jean Valjean, told by Victor Hugo, is too good to be true. When the good bishop met him there in that little home at night, a poor, hard, bitter, morose, savage, brutal man, and by a look of love and a single act seemed to transform a life, and brought him forth to a career of marvellous goodness, people think it too good to be true. Why, it is no more than Mr. Round tells us about that man who committed crime after crime, and who was hard and bitter and bloodthirsty, whom he helped time after time; yet one day while sitting in his office at his desk, he had the consciousness that some one was creeping up behind him. He rose to his feet, and there stood the man with murder in his eye and in his hardened face. Mr. Round stood there looking at him, and finally, with quivering lip, he said, "Jack, if you do that you will break my heart." And the man's face softened and the bludgeon dropped from his hand, and there began a new Valjean, a new life of righteousness and goodness. Why, there is not a minister in any of these cities anywhere, who has had wide experience, but could tell you of scores of cases like that man's transformation! The men and women down in the very worst slums of this city — those whom these men are seeking to win — are of infinite worth. They are, like ourselves, the sons and daughters of God. When we get that into our hearts, we will have money enough. When we can really get into the hearts of our church membership that the Lord Jesus longs and grieves and weeps over all these lost people, then we shall have money enough to carry the Gospel to them. But we need not only money: we need that the great heart of the church shall be anxious about this; shall be full of pleading for it; shall be full of heart-breaking sobs and tears for it; that the whole church shall be aroused to the fact that the one thing that Christ values in the world is to rescue these lost ones. When our church can show the same right to exist that the early church did — that we shall be everywhere seeking, at all times, to better the condition of the poor, soothe the fevered, clothe the children, better the wages and the comfort of all these men and women that are toiling against hope, and many times for months are pleading for a chance to toil — when we shall everywhere make the people believe by our actions, by our brotherly sympathy and fellowship, that the heart of the church is like the great heart of Christ, oh, I tell you we shall see glorious revivals! We shall see mighty triumphs in the city when that comes to pass!

There is nothing that palsies my heart like this, that Jesus Christ should be so much more popular among the non-churchgoing multitudes in our cities than our churches are. You can find man after man and home after home of the very sort I am talking about. I know you can find tens of thousands of men in this city who have great admiration for the name of Jesus

Christ and will shout for it, yet they do not have a feeling that the churches represent Him. I know, to a large extent, they have erroneous convictions on the subject, but down at the bottom there is something radically wrong that we have not come to feel how necessary it is for us to make everybody know that we are the disciples of Jesus, that "we have learned of Him." We ought not to care to be any more popular than Jesus Himself; we should wish to share His suffering, we ought to desire to share His sorrow, to share His humanity, and if Jesus were here and would find His luxury — yes, I repeat it — if Jesus Christ were here and would find His luxury in giving of His money and His time and all His thought and all His love and His sympathy in looking after and caring for the poor and the neglected and the out-of-work, and the people that are discouraged and disheartened, then, brother, we *must* find our luxury in doing these very things. We must not be above our Lord. We must put ourselves in our brother's place. You and I, standing here in these modern cities, represent Jesus Christ. Oh! God knows I preach it to myself as much as I preach it to you; the longing of my heart is that I may find what Jesus Christ would do if He were here. I do know that the great cities present the marvellous opportunity of our time; for it seems to me that there never was a time when these thousands and tens of thousands of oppressed and abused Russian Jews, and these poor half-hearted people, so far as religion is concerned, the Italians, who are coming to us — these multitudes, as sheep without a shepherd, half broken away from their own church ideas, sure to belong to Jesus Christ or the devil — were so ready to meet us, if we would meet them with open heart and sympathy, so ready to receive us and to receive our Gospel. O brothers and sisters, there never was such a mission field as these cities of ours right around the seaboard.

Talk about these people not being worth saving! Talk about a Jew not being worth saving, with the blood of Abraham and Isaac, and the blood of the Lord Jesus coursing in his veins! Talk about these Italians not being worth saving, with the blood of an Angelo and a Garibaldi, and the blood of the most marvellous painters and sculptors of the world filling them with life! All these people are coming to us with burdens, heart-broken and weary. What they need is a church standing in the place of the Master, saying in the tones of the Master, "Come unto me, all ye that labor and are heavy laden, and I will give you rest."

I shall never forget the impression I had once, when I sailed away from Holland in a Dutch steamer, watching the emigrants as they came on board. They were there from all around Holland everywhere — great, big, fat Dutchmen, who seemed to be as tall when lying down as when standing up. The old father and mother came down in many cases to bid good-by to the boy or the girl. It was a sorrowful crowd. It broke my heart as I looked at it. And after a while, when the cables were thrown off, and we began to get up steam and sailed out, there was a great waving of handkerchiefs of every color, and the old women waved their shawls, and some their bonnets and hats. And then for days afterward, all the way across, I noticed how sad that company was. We had almost reached this shore before they began to have a little courage again, and to brighten up with hope of the new land. They were homesick. I said to myself, "These people come over to us homesick and lonely and broken-hearted; and if we have the love and tenderness and sympathy of our Master, and we meet them with that spirit and with that tenderness and devotion — any church that will do that can win them and save them." And I pray God that New York Methodism will stand by this City Missionary Society. We must have greater devotion to these matters in our large cities. We must have united action.

We talk about the "great connectional spirit" in our denomination, about one preacher having an interest in all the churches. We ought to show to the world what a strong body like that can do. Every church in this city ought to be united in this great movement. It ought not to be left to a few noble-hearted men to carry this great burden alone. It is a shame that in these efforts in all our cities we almost break the backs, if not the hearts, of half a dozen great-hearted laymen that put their shoulders under the wheel. God bless these men! And He will bless them, I am sure. But what we need is that we shall stir every man and every woman — that we shall get the young people of the Epworth League interested in this work. My observation is that if you cannot get a man to give his money by the time he is thirty, or twenty-five even, there isn't much chance afterward. He gets miserly as he grows older. Let us appeal to our young men and young women; let us get hold of our children and youth; let us lay it upon their hearts that God intends for this generation to take the cities for Christ. We have no right to mortgage the future with our problems. If we are not able to take hold of this great question now, what right have we to believe that children born of such fathers and mothers as we will solve it? What right have we to leave it to them?

In my boyhood days beyond the Rocky Mountains, I read a sermon by one of those old pioneer saddlebag men. I tell you it was the man on horseback with his saddlebags who represented the romance and heroism of all my dreams in boyhood. He was one of those daring fellows, and the sermon was on the revolutionary spirit of Christianity. It had three heads. The first, The world is wrong side up; the second, It needs to be turned upside down; and third, *We are the men to do it.* We want that spirit now. Christ cares as much for us as for Paul or Peter. He is as willing to bless our words to-day as he was theirs. And when we get heart to heart with men, and go after them with tears, ready to be cursed ourselves rather than that they should not be won to God, we shall win these great cities to Him, and they shall become — New York city shall become — the kingdom of our Lord Jesus Christ.

www.ingramcontent.com/pod-product-compliance
Lightning Source LLC
Chambersburg PA
CBHW030430300426
44112CB00009B/936